Sketches in Democracy

Notes from an Urban Classroom

Lisa C. DeLorenzo

ROWMAN & LITTLEFIELD EDUCATION
A division of
ROWMAN & LITTLEFIELD PUBLISHERS, INC.
Lanham • New York • Toronto • Plymouth, UK

Published by Rowman & Littlefield Education
A division of Rowman & Littlefield Publishers, Inc.
A wholly owned subsidiary of The Rowman & Littlefield Publishing Group, Inc.
4501 Forbes Boulevard, Suite 200, Lanham, Maryland 20706
http://www.rowmaneducation.com

Estover Road, Plymouth PL6 7PY, United Kingdom

British Library Cataloguing in Publication Information Available

Library of Congress Cataloging-in-Publication Data

DeLorenzo, Lisa.
Sketches in democracy : notes from an urban classroom / Lisa DeLorenzo.
p. cm.
Summary: "Sketches in Democracy" is a captivating book that chronicles the first year in the life of a
new urban high school. Based on journal entries and educational literature, this book traces the
author's challenging journey toward creating a democratic community of learners within a tangle of
socioeconomic and political issues"-- Provided by publisher.
ISBN 978-1-61048-303-2 (hardback) -- ISBN 978-1-61048-304-9 (paper) -- ISBN 978-1-61048-305-
6 (electronic)
1. Education, Urban--United States. 2. Students with social disabilities--United States. 3. Democracy
and education--United States. I. Title.
LC5131.D37 2012
370.9173'2--dc23
2011045628

⊖™ The paper used in this publication meets the minimum requirements of American
National Standard for Information Sciences Permanence of Paper for Printed Library
Materials, ANSI/NISO Z39.48-1992.

Printed in the United States of America

With love, to my daughter, Molly

Contents

Foreword

Nicholas M. Michelli

I teach in a Ph.D. program in Urban Education in New York City. Needless to say, I am bombarded by books about education in general and urban education in particular. Many of them are theoretical socio-cultural discussions of society's ills reflected in urban schools as explanations for the crisis in education. Usually these books include a familiar list—poverty, crime, single-parent homes, drugs. I always ask, what are we to do with this list? The items may be explanations, in part, for what kids in urban contexts face, but the books seldom give us any guidance for what we might do.

Redistributing wealth and staging a revolution come to mind. Neither is likely in our lifetimes or that of our students—lifetimes in which we will see that there will be no majority, and the children we fail in urban schools will collectively be the majority. I always thought that what we needed was a book about urban schools that took into account the context, the theories, the difficulties faced, focused on what is needed and often missing from urban classrooms. A book that illustrated how hard the task of a teacher is, but left the reader with hope and some idea of what we might realistically do. I finally found that book in Lisa DeLorenzo's *Sketches in Democracy: Notes from an Urban Classroom.*

Of course the first thing one notices about this book is its title. What do sketches in democracy have to do with an urban classroom? In this day and age of increased regimentation, scripted curricula, test preparation, and high-stakes testing the idea connecting democracy with urban classroom seems incongruous to many educators and policy makers. But, as you will quickly see in these pages, democracy, and the preparation of students to live in a democratic culture *must* be present in urban and other classrooms. Why?

DeLorenzo clearly identifies the need to prepare all children to live in a democratic society if we are to continue to develop as a democracy. She does this, not with rhetoric, but with examples from her own classroom in a challenging urban setting. For example, in a chapter on "teachable moments" she states:

> A democracy is reciprocal and self-corrective, meaning that both people and the social structures sustain each other while always open to public scrutiny and evaluation. In a school, the reciprocal nature of democracy emerges from students and teachers working together in an environment of trust and respect. As self-corrective, a democratic classroom remains evolutionary; it allows for constant assessment of its effectiveness in providing joint decision making and equity among its participants.

Many might find such a statement in itself difficult to understand. In this book you will find that when an idea like this is presented, it is then followed with notes of a very personal nature from a real classroom. What principles of democracy can we expect teachers to teach? What do these actually look like? What worries and fears are teachers likely to experience? What happens if there is no support from the top, and moving in the direction advocated rests squarely on the shoulders of individual teachers? How do students behave?

Importantly, DeLorenzo does not allow us to equate teaching for democracy with unbridled freedom, as it sometimes is. Clearly this is a book about principled democracy. We know that in real life our freedoms must take into account the freedoms of others, and perhaps that is the limit of our own freedom—up to the point where it infringes on someone else's freedom. When children begin to understand that, and see how their behavior affects others' right to speak or express their point of view, the concept has real-world sense and its application to life can be made clearer.

There are so many important lessons to take from this book and I would like to highlight ten that seem to me to be important, but this is by no means an exhaustive list. They are just a few that I think you should look for as the reader, and you will find many more.

First, DeLorenzo promotes the idea of building a "community of inquiry" in each classroom, and suggests that all teachers be prepared to do so. She sees such communities as "precious, powerful" structures and "foundational for democratic practice." We see what that means, and that it is not an easy or linear practice. When the "community" exists and respect within the community for individuals and their contributions is engendered, learning occurs. Not only learning of the subject matter to be taught, but also, at the same time, knowledge of how individuals should behave toward their fellow participants in a democracy. Moving to this kind of community, she contends, takes us away from "playing school" and toward authentic learning. A powerful example is provided.

Second, DeLorenzo does not shy away from hard questions having to do with the role of White teachers in an essentially Black and Latino school. How does the "culture gap" between teacher and students play out? This is not an easy topic to confront without pejorative comparisons of "culture" which is of course unacceptable. How does someone like Lisa DeLorenzo describe and discuss the gap? Why, in the context of a Halloween party, of course! In the sketch used to examine this issue, teachers observe dancing that raises some concerns and confront the question of what, if anything, they should do. This is yet another inspiring example.

Third, feelings of "guilt" among White teachers are explored. No one I know has systematically examined his/her own feelings about being White in a classroom with Black kids so publicly. Do they despise me? Should I apologize for being White? Do my students know about the kind of racism that is likely to already be affecting them?

DeLorenzo uses her own field, music, to explore some of these questions. Is it the failure to provide art for all children in urban schools that explains the absence of black artists in premier American orchestras? How difficult is the path to being a professional musician or a music teacher? What would it cost? How far need we all go to be sure that students understand what they face? DeLorenzo adopts the view that we begin to be honest when we confront our own often unrecognized and perhaps unintended racism and, even more likely, the institutional racism that we know surrounds the places in which we work.

Fourth, noticing and taking advantage of teachable moments is an important point made very well in this book. Classrooms are very complex places, with hundreds of interactions likely in a single class session. If we are to seize upon unexpected teachable moments, how do we notice them? Do we abandon our plans? What kind of learning can occur? How far does a teacher go when the "moment" is likely to be very emotional? We find a coherent discussion and examples of taking advantage of these important opportunities that teachers probably encounter every day. How can teachers deal with pressure to "finish" the curriculum to be sure that students are ready for the test? What do we give up when that is the paramount purpose? How can teachers reconcile good teaching with administrative pressure that may not support good teaching?

Fifth, with statements like this, DeLorenzo creates a word picture that brings together much of what is important:

> Teaching for democratic practice, therefore, means that we look to the problematic as an opportunity for helping students broaden their vision beyond the immediate situation. It means that we value the potential of teachable moments within the recesses of a problematic situation. Most importantly, it means that we recognize the enormous growth potential from situations and issues that jeopardize students' rights to a safe, nurturing environment.

How do we look to the problematic? Why do we do so? What does it mean about our own values? How do we view our students if we are willing to stray from the scripted path to take advantage of opportunities for learning? If all teachers could do this I would feel much better about American public education. Readers of this book are challenged to imagine themselves in the role of an excellent teacher.

Sixth, what happens when there is a serious setback? Anything as complex as moving an urban school forward is likely to hit bumps. In one of the sketches here the teacher, DeLorenzo, finds that her students are falling back to behaviors they used at the beginning of the year, seemingly losing all the ground gained. Using a theoretical context she analyzes what is clearly a real situation and allows us to see how theory can help understand the situation and help determine the next move. Her next move is to focus on civil behavior—at least as important as civic behavior in a classroom and in a democratic society. What does it mean to be civil in our behaviors? How can we have students look at themselves and think about civility? Who is responsible for civility? DeLorenzo rightly contends that it cannot be the teacher who is ultimately responsible. The teacher can and should lay ground rules and help students understand behaviors, but then shifts the responsibility for civility and self-correction of uncivil behavior to the students. When that happens the battle is usually won, and a community emerges that is a place where learning can occur.

Reading these pages puts you in the hands of an expert teacher who does just that. It isn't that DeLorenzo doesn't have self-doubts, or doesn't wonder what in the world to do. She does. But then she analyzes the situation, matches it up with what she knows must occur—not for the moment but for the long-term preservation of civility and, yes, democracy itself—and puts the plan into successful action. What a treat it is to watch a talented teacher engage in this complicated and effective behavior!

As you will see the response was not shouting or showing anger, but rather showing empathy, nurturing, and caring, and actually expecting the same in return from the students. She invites the students to examine the class, essentially allowing them to take a macro view of what is happening, and suddenly, they understand. They know what was wrong, why the teacher was concerned, how learning and their futures can be compromised, and the ground lost is quickly regained.

Seventh, I think the book helps us understand what it means to be a professional teacher. Teaching as a profession has the advantage of having time that allows for reflection. From the outside it looks like time off. I used to cringe when teacher candidates said they were entering teaching to get summers off, reflecting the view that teachers have an easy job. Not so, says DeLorenzo. I would say professional teachers use that time to reflect, re-group, think about content and pedagogy and students, hone their skills and come back energized. Shulman has argued that a teacher with a class of twenty-five students has a far more complex job than a physician does with one patient. It is exhausting work when done right, even more exhausting when the context is less than supportive. Doing it without time to reflect is counterproductive. What does DeLorenzo come back with after reflection? You will see and understand what it means to model professionalism.

Eighth, DeLorenzo asks the question we should all try to answer: What does it take to have students want to learn? Every teacher in every discipline needs to answer this question. We should try to tell students why we they should study what we are asking them to study, but ultimately they must find out why themselves. The joy this teacher feels when the electronic keyboards arrive for her students is contagious, and these students can't wait to learn.

But it isn't just a matter of allowing them to go at it with earphones so no one else can hear. In this case DeLorenzo asks what can students learn about themselves and others by learning to care for a complicated instrument. She turns helping them understand appropriate behavior in the context of using an instrument into a vehicle for understanding another dimension of civil behavior. It turns out the students value the instruments and want them to continue to work. This becomes another triumph as they explore the possibil-ities and imagine what they will be able to do. And that is exactly how she starts a lesson—by letting them explore without preconceived goals or in-tended outcomes other than the opportunity to let loose and explore.

Imagine if we did that with all new ideas we introduce to our students? Then she moves from this experience to having the student watch a film of Beethoven struggling with his own life. Here, the students find a connection to themselves. How exciting it is to see high school students connecting with Beethoven! Of course finding an interest and using it as a window to the students' capabilities is known to be important, but what does it really look like? How do we get students engaged and then sustain that engagement? What do different levels of motivation look like? How does the level of motivation relate to focusing on a problem until progress is made? How does all this relate to a democratic society and preparing future participants in a democracy? DeLorenzo considers all of these questions, and you will be challenged to think about what you can do in your own classroom.

Ninth, the role of the arts in a democratic society and the importance of education in the arts for all students comes through loud and clear in these pages. Free expression is indeed the essence of democracy, and the arts are one very important means of expression. Whenever a society in history has moved away from democracy the censorship of the arts has been one of the first bits of evidence of the shift. If we care about democracy, we must care about the arts. Of course the other disciplines are important too, but the arts are endangered by the disproportionate focus on test outcomes in literacy and mathematics. In a budget crisis, it is often the arts that go first. The arguments in these pages for the importance of the arts should be required reading for every school board member and every citizen who votes for or against a school budget.

Tenth, we realize that the conditions needed for students to embrace democratic practice and learning are not enough. Those same conditions must be present for teachers. When important decisions that impact teachers' professional lives are made without their input, when simple supplies are not provided for teaching, when administrators do not understand the purposes of a school like this, there is little hope.

Like my own work and that of many of my colleagues, DeLorenzo's work is based on a few deeply held convictions about education. We must have faith in children and believe they can learn. If we don't they simply won't. It takes university faculty in education, in the arts and sciences, prekindergarten through grade 12 teachers and administrators, and the community working together to achieve success. When one of these elements is missing complete success is not likely to occur. All educators, K–12 and university, need ongoing, meaningful professional development to be effective in the long run. Our society must begin to understand the importance of education not just for the students we teach, but also for the long-term success of our society including its evolution towards becoming a fully formed and socially just democracy

So who is this person who I think has written one of the most important books in education to come along for a very long time? She is not a high school teacher. She is not a faculty member in a college of education. She is, instead, an accomplished professor in the arts and sciences—music to be specific—and a talented musician. How did she come to write this book? When the school she describes here was started, she decided to take a sabbatical from her university work to teach in the school and chronicle the first year. That in itself is an extraordinary commitment that few in her position would make. In fact, it may be unique for an arts and science faculty member, albeit one committed to excellence in K–12 education and its role in democracy in education, to leave the comfort of the ivory tower and spend a year in this school with these children.

Was the school successful? Did the school make a difference? You will see what she and her students think. No matter how we ultimately characterize the success or failure of the school, you will find here evidence that even in the most difficult situations, successes are possible and students' lives can be changed. The story told so skillfully here is an important case to analyze and understand for current and future K–12 faculty and administrators, for college faculty, for school boards, for policy makers and for the public. Because of Lisa DeLorenzo's commitment and work, we can do just that.

Nicholas M. Michelli is Presidential Professor in the Ph.D. program in Urban Education at the City University of New York Graduate Center.

Preface

Last day of school. I've been through many years of last days but none of them felt like this. In my first year of teaching, I cried as I watched the buses pull out with ecstatically screaming children waving goodbye. I didn't know how I would get through the summer without seeing "my kids" every day. One of the third grade teachers put her arm around me and said, "You'll get over this." The second year, when the buses pulled out, I felt a lump in my throat for about five minutes. The third year I waved once and skipped into the school to finish cleaning my room.

This year, twenty-some years later, was different. As my ninth grade students jostled each other out the door I felt nothing . . . no sadness, no melancholy, no relief. It had been the hardest year of teaching in my life. It had also been my most profound learning experience about teaching. At this small high school in the middle of an urban downtown, the students were as tough and raw as the maze of concrete sidewalks surrounding the school.

School was the least of their problems. Students accumulated absences from babysitting siblings for working parents. Lunches were missed for lack of money. Students were sick all the time, using the nurse as a substitute for a doctor who would charge more than the family could afford. Gangs courted some of the students. Sexual activity made lives all the more complicated for other students, four of whom became pregnant over the next summer. That very last day, before she walked out the door, the biggest, most difficult student walked over to me and said, "Dr. D., I just want you to know that you are the best music teacher I ever had." Thank God for that child. Thank God for all of them.

We can, if we choose, continue learning to teach at any stage in our career. Real learning—the kind that impacts your life over many years—is almost always painful and uncomfortable. Real learning involves a level of risk taking that places you on the precipice of succeeding brilliantly or failing miserably. Consider, for instance, the risk my former student took when she left her "teacher-of-the-year" elementary general music position to move across the state for a teaching position in high school choral music. "I'm really scared. What if I can't relate to the students? What if I can't make it? I am leaving everything to do this, but I just have to try and see whether I can teach in a high school situation."

Ironically, those were also some of my questions as I started the car for my first day at William Grant Still High School (a pseudonym). Having first taught music in an elementary school and then as a professor of music education at a medium-sized university, I had well over twenty years of experience as a teacher. What I didn't have, however, was experience teaching in an urban school.

The fact that I had only suburban and rural teaching experience, yet needed to prepare my university students for a highly diverse metropolitan area, left me feeling uncomfortably incomplete. As Kincheloe notes, "No one can go into urban schools to teach successfully without understanding and appreciating the everyday challenges many city students endure."[1] Thus, I applied for a yearlong sabbatical to teach music at an urban high school. I hoped to learn a lot about teaching in the inner city. My students made certain that I got those experiences.

William Grant Still High School (WGS) was born of a collaborative agreement between a nearby university and an urban school district. The university dreamed about a school that would serve not only as a place for preparing high school students to consider teaching as a career but also as a site for professional development, research, and active school reform. The school district initially agreed with these goals, leading to the formation of a school with a structure similar to that of a charter school.

Unfortunately, what seemed "mutual" at the outset often disintegrated into a political web of miscommunications and hidden agendas. This created a difficult environment for teaching, a condition not so terribly different from the conflicts that other urban schools often face. After four years, however, the partnership dissolved.

Given such a brief history, one might question the value of drawing information from a setting that, while founded on the best of intentions, fell through. This book, however, is not so much about the structural aspects of the school as it is about one year in the lives of its students and their teacher in an ongoing struggle to connect meaningfully and purposefully. Every school is unique and what we see in the particulars we can often generalize to the whole. That is, the stories of and from this school may have some details that are clearly specific to the setting, yet the underlying themes are germane to teaching and learning in schools throughout the country, especially in an urban context.

The themes in this book are taken from my journal written during that sabbatical year. The thematic content of the journal served as a springboard for exploring themes in teaching, teacher preparation, and democratic practice. Although music is my content area, this book is relevant to pre-service teachers, teachers, and teacher educators in all disciplines. In essence, this is a book about my experiences as a teacher in an urban school with special focus on educating future teachers.

One of the overriding themes addresses the challenge of democratizing education in an urban context where the infrastructure of urban schools, along with a societal culture of power, minimizes the students' growth as critically thinking, independent learners. John Goodlad, nationally known for his work on school reform, believes that schools are the only institutions specifically charged with enculturating our youth into an evolving democracy.[2] Such challenges are keenly felt in the urban schools.

The arts, in particular, bear the burden of public misunderstanding regarding their central role in the cultivation of democratic citizens. "The arts for inner city youths," Lakes states, "are democratizing influences reaching outward to new communities of individuals engaged in the creative process."[3] In *The Shame of the Nation,* Kozol writes,

> The virtual exclusion of aesthetics from the daily lives of children in these [inner city] schools is seldom mentioned when officials boast that they have pumped the scores on standardized exams . . . by drilling students for as many as five hours a day. The stripping away of cultural integrity and texture from the intellectual experience of children, denial of delight in what is beautiful and stimulating for its own sake . . . is a perennial calamity.[4]

Nevertheless, teaching as democratic practice spans all disciplines and all school contexts. And, whereas even with administrative support, suburban and rural schools struggle to define teaching practice that nurtures critically thinking students with a commitment to social justice, urban schools face a labyrinth of obstacles that make democratic practice difficult, but not impossible, to achieve. Consequently, this book not only explores thematic strands that emerge from everyday teaching but also seeks to examine them through a democratic lens with respect to teaching and teacher education. According to Ayers:

> As teachers we must fight for the central place of education in building our futures and in developing a robust democracy. Education and democracy are linked: A strong democracy requires a thoughtful, engaged, and active citizenry, and an education that encourages critical thought, reception and resistance, participation and empowerment, will push toward a more vital and inclusive democracy.[5]

It almost goes without saying that teaching in an urban community requires a special type of knowing. As with any school, teachers enter a dynamic system with its hierarchical power structure and political dimensions. Sooner or later, many teachers come to the realization that school is not just a collection of students, but rather a community within a community. The urban community has its own rhythm and lifeblood that pours into the schools on the heels of its students. It took many weeks for my rhythm to blend with those of my students. Eventually we found the groove, and sometimes . . . just sometimes, we were "smokin'."

NOTES

1. Joe L. Kincheloe, "City Kids—Not the Kind of Students You'd Want to Teach," in *Teaching City Kids*, ed. Joe L. Kincheloe and kecia hayes (New York: Peter Lang, 2007), 20.

2. John I. Goodlad, *Educational Renewal: Better Teachers, Better Schools* (San Francisco: Jossey-Bass, 1994).

3. Richard D. Lakes, "Urban Youth and Bibliographal Projects," in *Teaching City Kids*, ed. Joe L. Kincheloe and kecia hayes (New York: Peter Lang, 2007), 77.

4. Jonathan Kozol, *The Shame of the Nation* (New York: Three Rivers Press, 2005), 119–120.

5. William Ayers, *To Teach*, 2nd ed. (New York: Teachers College Press, 2007), xii.

Acknowledgments

I am indebted to those who have served as readers of my final manuscript: John I. Goodlad, Kristina Mann, Nicholas Michelli, Jennifer Ransom, Deborah Meier, Alison Reynolds, and Marissa Silverman.

I am also grateful to friends and colleagues who supported my writing throughout this process: Robbin Gordon-Cartier, Jennifer Robinson, Tina Jacobowitz, Nancy Tumposky, and Susan Nagle.

Thank you, as well, to my family for your unconditional love and encouragement as I worked on this book.

Chapter One

Birthing a School While Still in Labor

Teachers step into urban teaching for all kinds of reasons. Some cannot find jobs in suburbia. Others have a need to "save" those poor kids from the ghetto. And, some teachers, committed to social justice, see education as a means of providing children with the tools they need to find hope in an often ungracious world. These are the teachers whose wisdom extends far beyond the teaching of content to a deep understanding of the human condition and the important role that their students play in the process.

To become a teacher of urban students is a privilege that eludes many in our profession. Urban teaching has unquestionably received bad press: shootings, classrooms out of control, teacher safety, and so on. Except for extreme examples, such as Columbine, suburban schools seem to have much more balanced representation in the news. Nevertheless, the American psyche embraces the notion that bad things happen in urban schools.

Preparing teachers, then, becomes all the more challenging as it requires not just the teaching of skills and content, but also the development of heart and mind for marginalized students. Several years ago I decided that I could not authentically prepare my pre-service students to teach in urban schools if I had never had the experience myself. As luck would have it, a nearby university and urban public school district had just forged an agreement to jointly oversee a new high school academy.

It was a progressive but risky move for both the university and the district. For me, it was a sabbatical dream come true. Not only would I have the opportunity to teach for a year in an urban school but, more importantly, to participate in the birthing of the school during its first year of inception. On opening day, the school welcomed sixty ninth graders with the plan that each year another class of ninth graders would be added until the school reached its goal of grades nine through twelve. Although I expected to deepen my classroom experience, I never realized that I would actually learn to teach all over again. Consequently, this book is a reflective narrative that unravels what it means to test one's teaching, humble one's spirit, and question one's values on a daily basis.

William Grant Still High School (WGS) was housed in a large but defunct manufacturing building. Above the door, "Tile City," engraved in a crescent shape, remained its sole insignia during the school's first year. In the heart of the downtown district, the school was in a line of old, but architecturally beautiful stone-gray buildings. Everyone parked in a garage about three blocks away. Street parking was costly and risky; within the second month of school, one of the visiting university faculty members found her car sprinkled with glass from a smashed window.

Regardless, I never felt concern for my safety walking to and from the school. Some streets were littered with everything from limp paper bags to old used coffee cups. Other streets, however, were ardently cleaned by public service employees. There were good reasons to take caution (as in any big city) but few reasons to feel fearful. This is where my students hung out. This is where my students shopped. This is where my students lived.

Upon entering the actual school, a secretary's desk was positioned along the wall of a short narrow hallway. The renovation plans did not include a room for the secretary so she sat outside in the hall. (We went through three secretaries that year.) The school had four classrooms of different shapes and sizes, a coordinator's office, and a teacher's room. The small common space in the center included two large pillars, which quashed any idea of holding productive meetings with the student body.

The school, unfortunately, was more distinctive for what it didn't have than for what it had. As mentioned above, the school had no real space for congregating except in the classrooms. School-wide meetings were held in the largest classroom and students needed to bring their own chairs, creating a noisy chaotic beginning for the meeting. There was no gym, no science lab, no cafeteria, no library, no arts room, no computers, and no lockers. For physical education, students were bussed to a nearby YMCA, taught by a staff unprepared to deal with the age and needs of the students.

For science, lab work was conducted via textbook or other alternative means, like the day that each student got an owl pellet to dissect and find bones from the owl's lunch. As for library work, the students were on their own. They were expected to use community libraries near their homes, which usually meant long bus rides after dark. As computers began to arrive, students had less need for the library. The lack of arts space was especially disappointing but the school's constructed layout was obviously inadequate for much more than the four classrooms.

Lacking a cafeteria, students left the building to eat at a small high school across the street. To maintain safety while crossing the street, students were herded into a line while a teacher stopped the traffic. The nearby school's amenities, such as an enclosed courtyard, big airy classrooms, and modern architecture, were not lost on our students. In addition to a shared cafeteria, our school also shared a nurse and guidance counselor with other schools in the district. When illnesses or conflicts occurred on a no-nurse or no-counselor day the coordinator needed to call other schools where they worked and hope that they might arrive before too long.

Given many other published accounts of inner city schools,[1] these conditions may not seem extreme or noteworthy. However, this school was heralded as a special high school academy for students who wanted to be teachers. The initiators of this school included not only high-level administrators in the school district, but some of the strongest teacher educators in the university. In short, it was designed by teachers to serve as a model school for future teachers.

The WGS faculty included four full-time teachers, a full-time coordinator whose job was similar to that of a principal, part-time music specialist (my job), and a part-time art specialist. In addition, two professors from the university teacher education program served as liaisons between the school, the university, and the district administration. On Saturday, two days before the opening of school, contractors finally cleared the building for occupancy, but, without keys, none of the teachers had access to prepare their rooms for opening day.

> September 3: *Anxiety is high among the teachers at WGS. They have a classroom but no basic supplies such as textbooks, paper, pencils, etc. Consequently, our intelligent, highly motivated faculty feels a sickening sense that things, on the first day, might fall apart through no fault of our own and we will look bad for it.*

With trepidation, the faculty and students entered the newly renovated school for the first time. The entire school was eggshell white—the walls, the ceilings, and the hallways, which, although spotlessly clean, remained conspicuously naked of posters, welcome signs, or greetings. Classrooms were bare save for a few old tables, hurriedly moved from the top floors of the building and chairs (not enough for all the students).

Sixty impatient students milled around with wary eyes. They were quick to see the inconsistencies of old, beat-up furniture in contrast to the newly painted walls. Their street smarts told them that something was not right with this picture but their lingering hope held out for something that would explain all the discrepancies. Unfortunately we were waiting for the same thing.

September 7: *We clumsily guided all the students into a classroom built for*
fifteen with thirteen mismatched chairs. The room, as with the other rooms in
the schools, had no blackboards, desks, pencil sharpener, books, file cabinet,
or lockers. It was just a white empty shell with a few old worn-out chairs.

   Late as she was, the coordinator rushed into the room like a turbo engine.
She greeted the students with a loud commanding voice and proceeded to give
a lecture about rules, regulations, and disciplinary consequences. We stood
like paralyzed deer, each wondering how to construct a school based on
democratic practice when the coordinator had just modeled a traditional top-
down approach.

Unfortunately, her presentation as a controlling disciplinarian fit right into
the students' experiences of what a teacher should be. The students expected
to be told what to do and teachers who engaged in class discussions or
problem solving were seen as weak or not knowledgeable about their subject.
For these students who primarily lived in households where obedience rather
than independent thinking was the expectation, democratic values of shared
governance, critical thinking, and the rights of the individual versus the community had no place in the classroom—at least in their minds.

   One of the first activities in creating a democratic community is to have
students share in writing classroom rules or talk about their learning goals.
Theoretically, taking ownership over one's learning reflects a key component
in guiding students toward independent thinking. In our case, students interpreted these activities as a sign of teachers who didn't know what they were
doing. Even the terminology, "invite" and "share," must have seemed rudely
out of place in what students perceived as a school. While some of the
students played along, most found the morning activities strange or amusing.

Lunch was a circus. The first day had been set aside for a celebratory "pic-
nic" style meal with the whole group eating together instead of walking to the
cafeteria at the neighboring school. With no large meeting area to congregate,
the students set up some classroom tables in the central area of the building.

   Because the space was not large enough, they crammed into all of the
space available, often unable to pick up a drink without hitting another stu-
dent. Lunch consisted of a dry turkey sandwich and a choice of milk or juice
(still frozen). A number of students opted not to eat. By the end of lunch,
student behavior had eroded into loud talking, running to the bathroom, and
unsanctioned visitations with friends in other classrooms.

Music class was scheduled after lunch, promising classrooms of raucous,
hungry students. Given the events of the day, I could already see that my
carefully planned lesson was not going to work. As other teachers had discovered that morning, I faced a situation that had no viable solution other
than to salvage what I could from my now-not-appropriate lesson plan. Pre-
dictably, the students were bored and uninspired. At one point I asked stu-

dents how their first day had gone so far. Their immediate response was "dull, boring, and frustrating." Their complaints were embarrassingly legitimate. It was hard to imagine any of the students wanting to come back the next day.

Teachers often face situations that are not of their making yet they are still held accountable. A fire drill might interrupt a class discussion just as it starts to take off, an assembly program that coincides with an important test review session is not announced until that morning, the maintenance men show up unannounced to fix a leaky radiator, unpredictable announcements crackle over a high-volume intercom system, and so on. While such episodes become familiar interruptions for novice and experienced teachers alike, they still create a jolt in the teacher's plans and the students' learning.

The entire first day consisted of unexpected and unpredictable events at a time when it was paramount to establish routines and motivate students about interesting questions that posed intriguing issues for study. The cause of the infection, however, was of little consequence to the students who had already sized up the whole day as "we didn't get what we were promised."

In essence, the first day had been filled with broken promises both for us and for them. Although this was only day one, a tone had been set that had familiar resonance for urban youth who are constant survivors of disappointment. Right across the street was a beautiful, thriving school that literally hummed with purposeful activity. It took little imagination to see what our students didn't have.

At the end of the day, beleaguered and stunned, the faculty tried to come up with a workable plan for the following day. No one could have anticipated what it means to start a school from scratch, yet here we were, naively trying to build a democratic community without the least idea about how to do it. Fortunately, among the student body was a core of positive, optimistic adolescents who seemed willing to give the school a second chance.

Many critics would blame teacher education programs for failing teachers in their preparation for urban teaching. If "the curricula of university teacher education programs do not typically prepare teachers for the challenges of urban schools," then what do our beginning teachers need to know in order to succeed in urban teaching?[2] Moreover, given the disenfranchised nature of poor urban families, how do American teachers respond to the sense of urgency to empower their students as leaders in the community and stewards of democracy?

The typical teaching candidate is female, white, and without substantial personal experience with peers or teachers of different cultures. Most of these students come into the classroom with predispositions and stereotypical ideas that validate their reasons for avoiding urban teaching. The idea of teaching in the inner city, largely populated by people of different ethnic and racial backgrounds, is akin to stepping into a foreign country. And, in a sense, the urban culture is strikingly different when compare with the backgrounds of many students who enter teaching. For that reason, teacher education programs must work not only to teach skills but also to address the beliefs that students have about race, class, and schooling.

The education of teachers is a complex task made even more daunting when teacher education students have little field experience to serve as a frame of reference. For example, a typical methods class presents numerous teaching strategies that students might then use in their future classroom. Although the instructor can visually imagine the public school students, their responses, and a type of classroom structure, pre-service teacher education students have neither the range of experience with children/adolescents nor the day-to-day teaching process experience to fully connect college class activities with the public school classroom.

Nevertheless, new teachers might benefit from the following ideas. First, although the initial day at WGS posed a number of difficult and uncomfortable episodes, novice teachers do not learn about teaching from hearing scary teacher stories. While anecdotal stories, video clips, and readings serve a purpose in helping students broaden their vision of schooling, there is already enough exaggerated media coverage on urban schools to alarm would-be teachers.

Rather than stimulating productive conversation about teaching, frightening stories have the adverse effect, creating unnecessary anxiety that generalizes to misguided negative conclusions about teaching in urban schools. This is not to say that stories from the field serve little purpose. On the contrary, real-life stories help actualize the human side of teaching. It is important, though, to present stories in their full context where they have less opportunity to disguise themselves as universal truths about teaching.

Second, critics of education often berate universities for not training novice teachers for the real world. Inside the beginning teacher's head is a little voice screaming—"Just tell me what to do and how to do it." Yet, no school is exactly the same as another, creating one of the biggest disillusions in education of beginning teachers: *there are no universal solutions for the trials that teachers face, whether in urban, suburban, or rural settings.* Our reality of schooling is molded by our own experiential and cultural framework, which provides a context for talking about schools but rarely offers specific answers to generalized problems.

Third, in response to critics, there is no realistic way to prepare teachers for everything they may encounter at the school site. In general, teacher education programs are theoretical curriculums with embedded field experiences that provide a comprehensive but not all-encompassing preparation program for teachers. With the multitudinous number of teacher-student interactions, school structures, and parental/administrative encounters, it is unfair to hold teacher education programs accountable for every possible school configuration or human interaction. Classroom management, for instance, is probably the greatest source of anxiety for pre-service teachers. According to Ellsasser:

> New teachers are acutely aware of the classroom management challenges they will face. Understandably control is at the top of their list. They want strategies that will guarantee an orderly classroom. They look to their teacher-education professors for classroom management strategies. However the contextual and idiosyncratic nature of teaching defies such a prescriptive approach to teaching.[3]

These points aside, teacher education programs do have a moral obligation to prepare teachers with a reasonable perspective of what it means to teach in and for a democracy. Democratic practice recognizes that teaching is more than a content-driven enterprise. A healthy democracy relies on citizens who think critically, act responsibly, and commit to promoting a better society.

As teachers in the public sector, we have a greater purpose in teaching, not only developing intellect, but also advancing students' sensitivity to issues of social justice. Woodford suggests, "Democracy implies a loving concern for others and their welfare."[4] For the pre-service teachers who ardently believe that urban students have less to offer than suburban students, it is critical that their training address such ideas head-on. The ideals of democracy provide a meaningful platform for examining key issues of urban teaching: poverty, race, social and political participation, and the daily frustrations of simply moving through an average day in the life of an urban teenager.

For teachers, an integral step in democratizing one's classroom is creating a space that is open to conscientious probing of ideas. In Greene's compelling book, *The Dialectic of Freedom*, the author searches for spaces in American society where people can connect with one another to think, reflect, and imagine endless possibilities for elevating the human condition.[5] She calls for a discourse with the common good of humanity at its heart. A biology lesson on animal species, for instance, could focus solely on classification systems or it could extend into questions of social justice such as, "What are the long-term consequences for society when certain species become extinct?" From a teacher's perspective, this means that curriculum is rooted in a cultural/social context that relies on the teacher's skill to engage students in activities and discussion that deal with issues of equity, access to knowledge, appreciation for diverse points of view, and an awareness of the human condition.

No teacher can hope to accomplish these aims in a classroom where lack of trust and respect undermine the teaching/learning process. "Trusting relationships appear to be the first step in expanding and extending students' experiences."[6] Creating a climate of trust in an urban classroom, where students have every reason to distrust, becomes an immense and time-intensive task. Some of the barriers include a student's distrust of adults, a teacher's misunderstanding of cultural norms that affect behavior, the vulnerability of adolescents in searching for their place in the world, and the impact of socio-economic factors in a student's life.

These barriers remind us that students experience a complex of many different forces. Teachers must acknowledge these dimensions in order to fully grasp the factors that contribute to or challenge the formation of a democratically based classroom community. For that reason, building trust constitutes a major factor in a democratic community. Hopefully, university education classes have provided students with many authentic experiences in building trust between and among the students and instructor. Ensuring such experiences not only informs the beginning teacher's own work but also provides a context for pursuing the clash between beliefs and carefully examined ideas about teaching. At its best, a trusting community allows students to "imagine endless possibilities" for the education of citizens who think responsibly and have sensitivity to issues of social justice.

A democracy depends upon a delicate balance between examining issues of social justice and trusting in the capacity of citizens to engage in related problem solving. For decades, many schools have modeled quite the opposite paradigm: teachers as the questioners and problem solvers, students as receptacles for knowledge.

Freire refers to this as a system of bankers and depositories.[7] From an educational perspective, this dynamic creates a situation where students will always need a teacher to deliver information or to resolve a conflict. In a societal context, the banking system diminishes the power and right of people to think for themselves. The consequence, in its worst scenario, is a citizenry of oppressed and compliant individuals devoid of the tools for collective action in pursuit of the common good. In a school setting, this means that students have little to no opportunities for raising challenging questions or engagement in problem-situated learning activities. Repetitive worksheets and reliance on textbook-framed questioning/response narrow the possibilities for thoughtful discourse reflection, an element intrinsic to a thriving democracy.

With respect to the first day at WGS, any movement toward these ideals seemed futile. A democracy, however, is a process that evolves over time. The first day was just a beginning, albeit a rough beginning, toward building the kind of trust that results in healthy, empowered relationships.

First days of school are particularly fragile times for a beginning teacher: How will I introduce myself to my students? Will they like me? Should I develop the rules or should my students help me? Will they like me? Can I establish myself as the teacher in charge or will I come off as a bully? How can I make the first day fun while still setting a tone for serious work? Will they like me? Ladson-Billings remarks, "despite all of their youthful and idealistic enthusiasm, most new teachers are frightened and overwhelmed by the demand of teaching."[8]

The first day at WGS was disappointing for both the students and the faculty. From the time the doors opened to the end of the school day, our energy focused entirely on averting crises rather than setting a tone for compelling learning activities. What teachers can learn from days where nothing seems to go right is that another day is always coming. Rarely can a teacher, if acting in the best interests of the students, create an irrevocable situation. Perhaps the very best thing we can do for our pre-service students, aside from emphasizing flexible thinking, is to convey the fact that many events in teaching are caused by things beyond the individual teacher's control. As Ayers explains, "Teachers often work in difficult situations under impossible conditions. For the most part, your students are pretty forgiving—hopefully the teacher can forgive him/herself when things don't go as planned."[9]

Clearly, teaching as democratic process at WGS, or for that matter, any school, would not be easy. Whereas a democracy demands impatience with injustice, it also requires patience with its continual transformation. The success of school-based democracy relies on our belief in the integrity of the democratic process and the efficacy of that process in our students' lives. School students deserve more than a hastily written lesson plan or inert activities that underestimate the power of their ideas. They depend upon teachers to create a supportive community that engages them in essential questions about our world. This is the kind of school that we intended to build.

NOTES

1. See, for example, Jonathan Kozol, *Savage Inequalities* (New York: Crown Publishers, 1991).

2. Elaine M. Stotko, Rochelle Ingram, and Mary Ellen Beatty-O'Ferrall, "Promising Strategies for Attracting and Retaining Successful Urban Teachers," *Urban Education* 42 (2007): 42. doi: 10.1177/0042085906293927.

3. Christopher Ward Ellsasser, "Teaching Educational Philosophy: A Response to the Problem of First-Year Urban Teacher Transfer," *Urban Education* 40 (2008): 484. doi: 10.1177/0013124507304690.

4. Paul G. Woodford, *Democracy and Music Education: Liberalism, Ethics, and the Politics of Practice* (Bloomington: Indiana University Press, 2005), 58.

5. Maxine Greene, *The Dialectic of Freedom* (New York: Teachers College Press, 1988).

6. Catherine D. Ennis and M. Terri McCauley, "Creating Urban Classroom Communities Worthy of Trust," *Journal of Curriculum Studies* 34, no. 2 (2002): 152. doi: 10.1080/00220270110096370.

7. Paulo Freire, *Pedagogy of the Oppressed,* trans. Myra Bergman Ramos (New York: Continuum, 1990).

8. Gloria Ladson-Billings, *Crossing Over to Canaan: The Journey of New Teachers in Diverse Classrooms* (San Francisco: Jossey-Bass, 2001), 23.

9. William Ayers, *To Teach,* 2nd ed. (New York: Teachers College Press, 2007), 6.

Chapter Two

The Trouble with Mismatched Expectations

If one were to graph the comfort level of new teachers across the first school year, the line would start in the middle of the graph, then gradually dip lower and lower from October to December and begin to ascend sometime around January. It is the months between October to December when new teachers have exhausted their ideas from student teaching and their students are in the throes of deciding whether to work with or against them.

Certainly not all new teachers experience their first year in this way but, in general, there is a considerable period of time when the beginner's idealistic view of teaching runs up against the classroom wall. Expectations of what the teacher perceived as "real" teaching run counter to the realism of the job. It is this mismatch of expectations that causes anger, hurt feelings, and bewilderment. It is a time when many new teachers wonder why they went into teaching in the first place. It is also a time when new teachers are tempted to blame their teacher education program for poor preparation. Thus the realization that teaching is not always fun and "good teachers are not always fun" hits hard.[1] In the case of WGS, this downward dip started on day two.

September 8: *It seemed like the beginning of a good day. Although the students were reluctant to respond, eventually they came through. As we listened to different pieces of music, I was not surprised to find that students have such a strong personal connection to popular music on the radio but I was taken aback by their strong negative reaction to any other style of music, including jazz. In short, their definition of music was quite simple: rhythm and blues or rap. Everything else was laughable.*

As a side note, the students are amazingly unfettered by traditional social constraints or political correctness. They openly talk about white privilege, blacks, and Latinos without the "tread lightly" manner of adults. They proudly refer to themselves as "ghetto" kids.

Despite the success of the first two classes, the other two were much more difficult. The following behaviors contributed to troublesome classes:

1. *An overall malaise and apathy among the students—some students putting their heads down on the desk.*
2. *Constant interruptions and distractions during a discussion. The students seem unable to sustain dialogue without shouting out, interrupting their peers, clowning around, or giving absurd, inappropriate responses.*
3. *Students rarely build on what others say because they appear to have little interest in another point of view. Students often lapse into their own private conversations with friends.*
4. *There is tremendous lag time when transitioning from one activity to the next. For instance, when students needed to work in groups they were reluctant to physically move to another spot in the room, or did not hear the directions, or did not care about the directions.*

The lesson came to a halt somewhere in the middle of the period. Though the four classes showed differing levels of response to the lesson, the many forms of resistant behavior were overwhelming. My mental construct of urban ninth graders was completely off the mark.

Because WGS was a public high school "academy" and the students had to apply for entrance, we expected that the students would have a seriousness of purpose toward schooling and their studies. The faculty looked forward to dynamic and meaningful discussion with the students. In terms of music class, a unit built around themes of democracy posed opportunities for facilitating critical thinking through music literature. While all of these goals were possible, the students had more pressing needs at that point in time (e.g., a sense of order and community).

September 10: *What I am finding, in reality, is that students see music solely as a time for fun and resent having to think about it. Perhaps I should have capitalized on the fun part right away instead of approaching music with such weightiness. Why hadn't I realized this fundamental principle? I guess I thought that if music was too much fun, the students wouldn't take it seriously. Guess what? They don't take it seriously anyway so why not seize the opportunity to have fun and hook their interest as a bridge to other material? Or better yet, why not see their musical choices as a socially relevant springboard that gives more authentic direction to the music curriculum.*

Eleanor Roosevelt said, "It is easy enough to impart book knowledge, but it is not so easy to build up the relationship between youth and older people."[2] As good teachers know, building relationships is integral to the teaching/learning process. Learning cannot take place unless students respect the rights of all participants. Although curriculum also plays a major role, it seemed a distant second to our struggle in connecting with students.

Herein lies another disillusionment in teaching: As long as the lesson plan is engaging and relevant, the students will become immersed in the process. It is difficult to let go of this myth when all through college one is usually rewarded for hard work. According to Haberman, though, successful completion of the first year in teaching has nothing to do with "having been 'successful' in a college preparation program."[3] When a teacher extends an invitation to learn something new, the student may not always accept that invitation. In fact, sometimes students don't accept our invitations until long after they leave our classrooms.[4]

Of all teachers, the beginner is most vulnerable to fear of failure—fear of not knowing what to do, fear of student rejection, and, most of all, fear of discovering that teaching might have been a huge career mistake. All of these doubts cast a shadow in the minds of those who confront crises every day. Whereas more experienced teachers have a track record of teaching that lends some measure of assurance in the process, first-year teachers are in the initial stages of constructing their own self-concept as teachers. For this reason, the neophyte teacher can easily magnify any student disagreement or verbal assault to a level of distortion that quickly diminishes self-esteem.

Accordingly, statistics tell us that about 14 percent of public school teachers leave after their first year of teaching with nearly 50 percent leaving after their fifth year.[5] The percentages in urban schools are even higher. Factors that contribute to the pathology of urban schools include inexperienced and inadequate teachers, culturally irrelevant curriculum, low expectations, and excessive use of punitive measures. Such factors, commonly cited in the literature, also contribute to the high rate of teacher flight from urban to suburban schools.[6]

Just as a democracy rests on firmly held tenets that are open to continual scrutiny and examination, so must teachers operate from a set of deeply held beliefs that frames their decision making. Without a philosophical core in place, teachers are at risk of becoming pawns in the classroom. Expectations about what teaching should be, in conflict with opposing circumstances of the actual job, contribute to the failure that some teachers feel early on.

Consider the following spiral of events: A teacher begins his/her first year with energy and anticipation; the students, however, assume the position of power as the more experienced agents in the school; a battle for control renders the teacher feeling defensive and needing to put students back in their place; negotiating becomes the norm as teachers use more and more extrinsic rewards or threats to achieve control; and, discipline takes center stage over teaching/learning, giving students a reason for responding with apathy or rebellion. Teaching then becomes reduced to little more than behavior management. [7]

"Dangerous Minds," for example, is one of many teacher hero movies that portray a neophyte teacher trying to cope with a disorderly, unmotivated group of students. In this movie a beginning English teacher, played by Michelle Pfeifer, is hired to teach troublesome urban high school students who have no more interest in learning about literature than they do about coming to school. Typically the story line centers on a gradual building of trust among the students who, in the end, become respectful and protective of the teacher and the subject matter.

In one scene the teacher gains control and affection by throwing candy bars to students who participate. A knowledgeable educator would understand that such bribes are short-lived and only lead to a need for bigger bribes. With the many movies that feature teacher-wins-students, it is tempting to lose sight of the fact that films are made for audiences and that in the search for dramatic material, realism is not the main purpose.

Unfortunately, vivid film scenes often become vehicles for misinterpreting what a good teacher does to earn the trust of his/her students. Rarely do we see the arduous process of building relationships where teachers gain ground in small increments over a long period of time. Nor should we expect that an individual teacher could fix a system that is inherently flawed. Accordingly, Ayers, Ladson-Billings, Michie, and Noguera write:

> We resist the image of the hero teacher. First, because it operates in the patronizing conceit of child saving . . . and second, because it denigrates the steady commitment of hard-working teachers who don't experience daily miracles in their classrooms. But, most of all, we oppose the hero-teacher notion because it perpetuates the lie that the only thing needed to bring about equality of opportunity and outcomes in city schools is a caring individual—a nice white lady. [8]

Experienced urban teachers have firsthand knowledge of the challenges involved in meeting students' needs and set appropriate boundaries to accomplish this. An important question for teacher education programs, then, centers on how one prepares neophyte teachers for teaching in an urban school without unconsciously triggering the "rescuer" fantasy that movies tend to project. It is acknowledged, but often overlooked, that pre-service teachers' fears about violent, unmanageable students remain at the forefront of their thinking. This mindset is often reinforced through the sensationalism of stories in the media, family members, and friends without teaching experience themselves. Consequently, the challenge for teacher education programs lie first, in mediating those fears and second, in developing sensitivity to the cultural, ethnic, and other needs of their students. [9]

Because good teaching flows from a deeply held philosophy of learning, teacher education programs engage students in constructing their own teaching philosophy. Most often this constructed philosophy reflects beliefs appropriate to a suburban school setting. Ellsasser feels, however, that this exercise does not target the specific needs of the urban student. The purpose in reflecting on the urban student, he believes, is to think through the unique issues of urban teaching right from the start. "Such an approach to educational philosophy is particularly important for teachers . . . who are likely to find themselves being subjected to a system and norms of behavior that threaten to diminish rather than enhance their professionalism." [10] When also grounded in democratic ideals, it would seem that a philosophy for urban teaching gains strength and social relevance for beginning and experienced teachers alike.

Sometimes constructing a teaching philosophy takes place before students have had sufficient experience with the urban setting. At the university, for instance, many teacher educators present teaching strategies with the tacit assumption that most school students have fairly well-developed habits of schooling such as staying in their seats during instruction or following directions. They tend to model lessons for hypothetical teaching scenarios in highly controlled settings because, frankly, it is impossible to create an authentic classroom with a group of college students. The upshot is that without consistent field experiences in the urban setting, pre-service students get most of their university teaching experience geared toward a suburban setting.

Whereas the work of experienced urban teachers contributes to the sophistication and "realness" of their philosophy, pre-service teachers begin their program with little to no context from which to formulate a philosophical framework. A few observations or discussions about teaching cannot substitute for the visceral learning that takes place when pre-service teachers step into the public school and begin to interact with the students. It goes without saying that students who have only observed or interned in suburban settings have no base from which to construct an urban-centered philosophy.

When teachers in the classroom feel like they are drowning, the very idea of philosophy as a life rope seems idealistic and overly academic. What teachers want are strategies, quick fixes, anything to stop the continual hammering of student discontent. First-year teachers suffer tremendously when their university-developed philosophy and training do not to mirror their professional situation.

Despite four or five years in the college classroom engaging in discussions about learning and participating in model activities where peers do all the right things, first-year teachers may find that suddenly nothing goes the way it is supposed to. It takes very little, under such circumstances, to fall into nonproductive teaching behaviors, for example, abandoning group projects in favor of mindless worksheets that get immediate results and fit in with the style of other faculty who may not model effective teaching. The impulse to revert to yelling, reward tokens, or blaming students for the problem ("If we just got rid of Sam, the class would be so much better") becomes a dangerous fallback to the frustrated, at-the-end-of-my-rope novice. When novice teachers begin teaching with unrealistic expectations, the mismatch between what some teacher education programs present and what novice teachers actually need can magnify feelings of failure or helplessness.

Mismatched expectations between the teachers and students at WGS accounted for much of the difficulty in the initial stages of building a program. When preparing for classes, we assumed that students would, for example, come to school on time, stay in their seats during a lesson, and make an effort to do their homework. In our mind's eye, episodes of disruptive behavior were short and easily contained. At WGS, however, about 30 percent of the students did not demonstrate those standard habits of schooling. Their style of discourse was not only different from ours but their attitudes may also have been shaped by a distrust of adults, a lack of concern for school procedures, and/or a lack of respect for themselves and others.

The students seemed to push unwanted behaviors to their fullest extent. The lack of common courtesies, however small, such as saying "Good morning," or not recognizing the need to help a teacher struggling to carry a piece of equipment, represented the norm. Filtered through our suburban lens, the students left many of us speechless and baffled. One day in October, for instance, a student walked brazenly into my classroom and handed a note to her friend while I was teaching. When I explained that she had just distracted the entire class, she looked annoyed and puzzled as if to say, "What's the matter with you?" She sauntered out calling, "I had to give Keesha a note— OK?" (She clearly wasn't asking for my permission.) None of us expected these types of behavior and therefore had no procedure or philosophical anchor in place for addressing small or larger incidents.

How were the other teachers in WGS faring during this period of time? Much of the day was spent shifting from pleading to screaming. Some of the teachers fell into a pattern of requesting quiet, trying to discuss behavior with students, and then yelling for order. Tony's classroom was quiet. Tony taught in a traditional format where the teacher delivers instruction and students take notes. His class was well managed through lectures, videos, and seatwork.

For those who believe in active, hands-on learning, Tony's strategies conflicted with the nature of a democratic classroom. Paradoxically, the other teachers' as well as my own efforts to build democratic classrooms were no more illustrative of student-centered learning or productivity than his. Classroom management seemed as futile as managing a brush fire in the wind. While one fire flared in the back of the room, sparks were already igniting in the front of the room. Although the standard axiom, "I will just wait until you are ready," may be effective in some classrooms, students typically interpreted the wait as "I have unlimited time to talk with my friends because the teacher will just wait." Without clear boundaries on behavior, democratic practice cannot take place.

In professional development and practitioner articles, we often learn that developing self-control outweighs the short-term benefits of threats and punishments. "Students are far less likely to act aggressively, intrusively, or obnoxiously with teachers who concern themselves less with controlling behavior and more with student learning."[11] When these hard-and-fast beliefs form the foundation of one's teaching philosophy, it is unnerving to see students behaving so noisily and rudely. In this case, the teacher's conception of schooling collides with the students' conception of how a school should run.

One day, with a particularly difficult class, I stopped the lesson and asked the students to get out a sheet of paper. They assumed I was about to give a pop quiz. However, I explained that the classroom chaos had reached a place of no return. "I need you to help me figure this out. So, please use that paper to write me a letter with your ideas about how we can have a more peaceful classroom." Most of the letters were surprising. Instead of negative comments about the class, many letters were apologetic, offering various ways of punishing the offenders for their crimes. One letter, from the smallest, quietest child, chilled me: "Dr. D., if you want to gain respect you will have to beat us."

This depressing note revealed something important about expectations—that although we may have a vision of democratic schooling, the students wanted what was most familiar to them: authoritarian instruction, a highly punitive environment, and a setting that used humiliation and intimidation as controlling mechanism—familiar characteristics in many urban schools.[12] The students were more comfortable in an environment where someone told them exactly what to do than in an environment that offered student decision making and responsible participation.

WGS came to fruition with a belief in school-based democracy, a structure that would involve students in meaningful decision making about their learning and their community. It was intended that curricula would cover a broad range of themes, cultures, and learning styles in concert with issues of social justice. We anticipated that informed discussions would serve an important role for giving students an equal chance to participate as well as to develop the self-discipline in listening to other's perspectives.

Ironically even the faculty did not begin the school year with a collective vision of what a democratic school should look like. This, and the colliding expectations of district administrators, led to constant controversy about how to manage the school. Whereas the school district wanted teacher-directed classrooms and high test scores, the university wanted a school that modeled democratic practice as a laboratory for teacher education students. The teachers wanted to focus on group projects and portfolios. And, the students thought they wanted a teacher as the decision maker, the punisher, and the dispenser of information.

Regardless, any semblance of democratic practice cannot sustain itself under conditions where neither the students nor the teacher are working toward a common purpose. First, a democratically based school has a well-developed mission embraced by all. Second, this mission reflects the importance of students, school personnel, and a parental community involved in the academic and social design of the school. This kind of mission had yet to evolve at WGS.

Without a common starting place, launching a school based on democratic principles presents an arduous challenge, especially when the school, the administration, and the community have opposing expectations. How, for example, does one begin to construct a democratic climate with students whose mode of life is characterized by arguing, fighting, and bullying to maintain self-respect? Moreover, how do we build a democratic foundation in a community where families are frequently marginalized from mainstream decision making? Nothing in the urban setting comes easily and, in terms of democratic practice, "exercising democracy involves tensions and contradictions."[13]

If there is one outstanding quality that urban teachers must possess it is perseverance. In the face of administrative bullying and faculty opposition, critical pedagogy will always feel like swimming upstream. Any renewal efforts along the lines of democratic practice are fraught with agonizing decisions and political inconsistencies. Meier warns us, "It is sometimes easier to complain about an unfair system than to be a powerful member of a tough profession."[14]

We must also recognize that when beginning teachers face tests of perseverance, such tests often come at a time when they are the most vulnerable, least unsure, and most willing to grab any lifeline that offers relief. We learn perseverance by tenaciously holding on to what we believe in the face of formidable circumstances. Because perseverance is such a critical disposition in urban teaching, teacher education programs must find ways to address this.

Perseverance cannot be directly taught but emerges from personal experience coping with thorny obstacles. Hopefully, most pre-service teachers will have experienced what it means to persevere during a difficult time at some point in their life. Some students may remember a personal incident in which they had to withstand the bullying of another student. Others might think about a difficult assignment that took several weeks to solve. Drawing on these powerful feelings and connecting them with specific teaching situations are one way of addressing perseverance. Even better, students learn to persevere when they engage in tutoring or other experiences that involve sustained interaction with a child over a number of weeks or months. It is the teacher educator, then, who builds upon these feelings of perseverance to discuss positive ways of coping with difficult situations in the teaching process.

Beginning teachers enter the profession believing that teaching is a straightforward line toward that symphonic spot where everything falls into place and one has finally arrived. But teaching is not linear and never really arrives at the point where you finally feel like you know exactly how to do it. The composer Mendelssohn wrote that music is always in a state of becoming. As with music, teachers, students, and schools reflect that same evolutionary nature. Coming to terms with this dynamic concept of schooling is one step closer to recognizing the democratic potential of education.

The democratic potential at WGS was strong. Yet, looking back at this difficult time, one sees an incompatibility between what was happening at the school and the conditions necessary for democratic practice. Mismatched expectations about these conditions, whether emanating from an irrelevant teaching philosophy or reflected in the unsupportive behavior of students, create serious but not insurmountable roadblocks in working to build a democratic school. Perseverance and tolerance for short-lived instability, however, become requisite dispositions in moving this agenda forward.

"If you want respect, you have to beat us." Eva came from a school overseas where corporal punishment was an expected part of the school day. In her eyes, there was nothing wrong with smacking a ruler in the palm of some offender. It worked quickly and effectively. What's more, it had an intimidating impact on the rest of the class—creating the quiet, well-mannered classroom that she had rarely experienced at WGS. Clearly, beating children was not an option, unthinkable at best. However, knowing that democracy is a transformative process that doesn't happen all at once offered hope that sometime soon, the students would begin to feel the power of working together as a community.

NOTES

1. William Ayers, *To Teach,* 2nd ed. (New York: Teachers College Press, 2007), 12.

2. Allida M. Black, ed., *What I Hope to Leave Behind: The Essential Essays of Eleanor Roosevelt* (Brooklyn: Carlson Publishing, 1995), 304.

3. Martin Haberman, *Star Teachers of Children in Poverty* (West Lafayette, IN: Kappa Delta Pi, 1995), 2.

4. William Watson Purkey and John M. Novak, *Inviting School Success,* 2nd ed. (Belmont, CA: Wadsworth, 1984).

5. Alliance for Excellent Education, *Tapping the Potential: Retaining and Developing High-Quality New Teachers* (Washington, DC, 2010). http://www.all4ed.org/files/Tapping-ThePotential.pdf.

6. Catherine D. Ennis and M. Terri McCauley, "Creating Urban Classroom Communities Worthy of Trust," *Journal of Curriculum Studies* 34, no. 2 (2002): 152. doi: 10.1080/00220270110096370.

7. Christopher Ward Ellsasser, "Teaching Educational Philosophy: A Response to the Problem of First-Year Urban Teacher Transfer," *Urban Education* 40 (2008): 484. doi: 10.1177/0013124507304690.

8. William Ayers, Gloria Ladson-Billings, Gregory Michie, and Pedro Noguera, eds., *City Kids, City Schools: More Reports from the Front Row* (New York: The New Press, 2008), xxvii.

9. Dave F. Brown, "Urban Teachers' Professed Classroom Management Strategies: Reflections of Culturally Responsive Teaching," *Urban Education* 39 (2004): 266–289. doi: 10.1177/0042085904263258.

10. Ellsasser, "Teaching Educational Philosophy," 483.

11. Alfie Kohn, "Beyond Discipline," *Education Week* (November 20, 1996): 3. http://www.alphiekohn.org/teaching/edweek/inwwt.htm.

12. See, for example, Gaston Alonso, Noel S. Anderson, Celina Su, and Jeanne Theoharis, *Our Schools Suck: Students Talk Back to a Segregated Nation on the Failures of Urban Education* (New York: New York University Press, 2009); Jonathan Kozol, *The Shame of the Nation* (New York: Three Rivers Press, 2005).

13. James A. Beane and Michael W. Apple, "The Case for Democratic Schools," in *Democratic Schools*, ed. Michael W. Apple and James A. Beane (Alexandria, VA: Association for Supervision and Curriculum Development, 1995), 8.

14. Deborah Meier, *In Schools We Trust: Creating Communities of Learning in an Era of Testing and Standardization* (Boston: Beacon Press, 2002), 95.

Chapter Three

Playing School Is Not the Real Thing

When issues of behavior management take a front row seat in the daily life of the classroom, it is easy to become discouraged with the ideals of democratic practice. The decision to build a democratic community of learners is, perhaps, the most challenging part of the process. Unfortunately, teacher education programs and professional development workshops tend to present strategies or ideas for teachers who already have a healthy community of learners in place. Such assumptions overlook the sheer complexity of developing a community from the very beginning.

The concept of learning communities is not new to education. However, we often use the term "learning communities" loosely as if any group of students (or teachers) constitutes a community of learners. Learning communities differ from other groups in that they reflect people in mutual cooperation held together by a common learning interest or goal. According to hooks, "Seeing the classroom always as a communal place enhances the likelihood of collective effort in creating and sustaining a learning community."[1] One can think of a learning community as the class, groups within the class, teacher study groups, or the school itself.

Essentially, a learning community implies a shift from membership by default (e.g., a student in a school) to a group in which each person's contribution is considered and valued with respect to the good of the whole (i.e., the common good). The idea of working together for the common good not only provides the grounding for a productive learning community but also is fundamental to a democratic environment. A distinguishing feature of democratic classrooms, then, lies in the emphasis on cooperation and collaboration rather than competition.

In building learning communities, sometimes teachers get tangled in the idea of democracy as unrestrained freedom, not knowing when to demand and when to pull back. The initial tendency is to pull back too much. Because freedom and democracy are so tightly intertwined, teachers may forget that freedom relies on responsible behavior and reasoned judgment making. It is impossible for democracy to take root when students have no basic sense of purpose and order in the classroom.

Questions of how to create freedom with boundaries are intrinsic to a learning community and democratically based school. How does a teacher share control without losing control? How much student decision making is appropriate before it overshadows the teacher's right to guide the learning process? Consequently, issues of authority and control stand in delicate balance with student-centered problem solving and discussions.

Along with the issue of control and freedom, other factors affect the formation of a classroom community. Students, at the start of school, are initially confronted with the social dynamics of a new class. As students attempt to find their place in a classroom community they face struggles for popularity, the perceived judgments of other students, and a need to belong. This directly influences the feeling of safety that is germane to building a productive community of learning.

Without the support of administrators or other teachers, building communities of learning becomes even more difficult. Some may even view democratic practice as subversive because the emphasis on student problem solving and discussion does not fit the traditional model of teacher-directed instruction. This is not to say that teacher-directed instruction is "anti-democratic" but that it has its place *along* with student-centered activities. A school that values the development of learning communities provides the support teachers need for a variety of teaching modalities.

Trust and mutual regard are critical elements in a learning community. Although most of the teachers at WGS valued learning communities, we had yet to develop trusting relationships with the students. Students continued to behave in ways counterproductive to an effective learning environment and the faculty struggled to keep abreast of daily crises. In effect we were "playing" school rather than "doing" school. In other words, we were going through the motions of democratic practice without truly building a democratic culture.

October 6: *Starting a class is particularly painful because the students are skilled at pretending not to notice when a change of teachers has taken place. As I stand amidst the commotion, a few students get irritated and start screaming "shut up" which doesn't exactly set a good tone. When I finally have some attention and launch into the music lesson many students resume their previ-*

ous activities of talking, writing notes, putting on make-up, etc. Unbelievably, some students even bring their photo albums to share with friends during class.

The kind of school that we envisioned called for students to have trust and respect for each other. To us that included understanding the difference between contributing to a discussion and interrupting a discussion. They needed help in developing impulse control and understanding that yelling and calling out disrupted everyone. In short, the students needed habits of behavior that would lead to psychologically safe spaces for learning.

Learning communities provide academic support as well as dispositions for learning. In a learning community, one would generally see discussion, group projects, and a constructivist approach to learning. Whereas most WGS faculty leaned toward these activities, the students were used to a top-down approach: the teacher lectures and the students take notes. Not only did the school district favor the top-down approach; this approach also pervaded some family structures where discussions were seen as disrespectful. For some of our students the primary mode of communication, within the family, rallied around yelling and commanding rather than listening and responding.

Our small classes, numbering fifteen students, should have provided unparalleled opportunities to know our students and their needs on a more personal level. Yet in this ideally structured school, students responded more readily to worksheets or videos than substantive discussion and collaborative tasks. There were moments, however, when students showed interest and excitement in their learning. When this happened we reveled in the hope that we had finally found a way to connect with the students. In reality, the connections were tenuous. Classroom management problems as well as the personal problems of individual students depleted our energy. Kopetz, Lease, and Warren-Kring[2] write:

> We know that the concerns of teachers are real. The sense of frustration, the anger, the feeling of helplessness evoked by the following words echoed through the halls in every school we entered: "How can we do anything? Every child has these problems. It's not just once in a while; it is every day. If we deal with these issues, we won't ever get to teaching!

Two themes that appear consistently throughout the educational literature are the importance of cultivating trust and the need for culturally responsive teaching.[3] These intertwined themes speak to the unmitigated importance of the student-teacher relationships. Without mutual regard for one another, any movement toward building productive learning communities is futile.

Trusting relationships are not only central to learning communities but integral to the process of democratizing a school. Ennis and McCauley state, "The reluctance to trust often leads to the unraveling of the goodwill that serves as the foundation for a learning community."[4] A good school builds many layers of trust, ranging from student and teacher relationships to the public's trust that schools will provide excellence in instruction.[5]

In their informative study, "Creating Urban Classroom Communities Worthy of Trust,"[6] Ennis and McCauley examined characteristics of urban high school teachers selected for their exemplary work with difficult students. The researchers identified mutual trust as the single most essential characteristic in working with troubled students. "Although there may be a tendency to think of trust as a peripheral aspect of the school environment, we contend herein that trust is, or should be, at the centre of the school experience."[7] Further, "Students are more likely to expend effort when they think the teacher is interested in them and makes the content meaningful in their lives."[8]

Trust begins to materialize when teachers and students share similar expectations. Incompatible expectations about the learning process inhibit the growth of collaboration and cooperation. Part of building trust involves seeing the student within his/her cultural context. This kind of knowing goes beyond geographic location (e.g., a student from Colombia) and suggests that teachers must also come to know the student's communication patterns and view of the world. Ladson-Billings has written extensively about the impact of culture on student learning and relationships:

> Culturally relevant teachers know that it is their job to learn about students' cultures and their communities . . . They do not assume that students have to learn their ways and rules. They understand that the interest they show in students' backgrounds and lives have an important payoff in the classroom.[9]

Cultural responsiveness means that teachers recognize the significance of selecting culturally relevant material and designing strategies that take students' culture into account. In language arts, for example, it is crucial to include authors of color. In the social studies class, teachers should credit the valuable contributions that persons of color have made to the development of our country. These are not token references but stories woven into the fabric of the history and culture of our country. Teachers invested in culturally responsive teaching "see themselves as part of the community and they see teaching as giving back to the community."[10]

A big part of knowing the student involves knowing the family context and the community. This is especially important as teachers and administrators generally live outside the community. At WGS the faculty racial makeup and socio-economic status differed extensively from those whom we taught. We neither lived in the community nor, at this point in the year, had meaningful relationships with parents. Whereas each of us applied for this teaching assignment with the strong desire to teach urban youth, the racial and class distinctions could not help but magnify the differences between our students and us. As Anyon remarks, "social class and race often differentiate them [teachers] from students, families, and other residents."[11]

The family culture, as well as that of the community, has a powerful role in shaping the students' values and coping mechanisms.[12] Through a White lens, however, urban families and communities are often blamed as part of the problem rather than part of the solution. It is easy to operate under the assumption that the school and the family have separate lives—except when problems arise in the classroom. It is equally convenient, but unfair, to rationalize that dysfunctional family structures are solely responsible for the problems in the urban schools. In fact, Theoharis's research reveals that most urban students want to make their families proud, refuting the idea that "parents are not sufficiently committed to their children's education and contribute to a 'culture of failure' among urban students."[13]

Coming to know the family is an investment that the teacher makes in order to better reach his/her students. In reality, the process is not so cut-and-dried. The complexity of family relationships often presents communication obstacles for both teachers and caretakers. Language barriers make communication especially difficult. Other examples include students who live in different families but share the same father or mother. This is particularly problematic when both students are placed in the same class. Sometimes, a parent will leave his/her child with a relative in order to return to their country of origin for great lengths of time. In one case, the student was homeless and lived in a shelter. The day I brought my adopted Chinese four-year-old daughter to class, Shariff wanted to know, "What mix is she?" In other words, what was her racial makeup? Classmates of a mix of several races are so commonplace that the question seemed as ordinary as asking "How old are you?"

Building trust, along with cultural responsiveness, takes time.[14] In thinking about these beginning months at the school, I am struck by the tension between urgency and patience. The faculty had wonderfully creative ideas for learning projects but underestimated the complex network of relationships that anchor a productive learning community. In our impatience to teach content we misread the cues coming from our students—that this school was unlike any they had ever encountered and they had neither the skills nor familiarity with ways of learning that this school promoted.

Along with this, the faculty came to the realization that we didn't know much about each other. Each of us was a new teacher to the school, with a new head teacher, in a new building, within a new community. Meier, the founder of several successful small, urban schools states, "The staff must know each other well, be familiar with each other's work, and know how the school operates."[15] Fortunately, as time passed and we started to collaborate on learning projects, this "newness" started to wane.

One afternoon we had an in-service joint workshop that included the students as well as the faculty. During the workshop, the facilitator asked how many of us had experienced the murder of a friend or family member. It was horrifying to see how many student hands shot in the air. Next the facilitator asked, "How many of you think of yourselves as Black . . . Latino . . . White?" The disparity between our White faculty and students of color was painfully obvious.

It is no secret that students of color reflect the total, or near-total population of urban schools. In fact, several writers present well-articulated arguments that American schools have become segregated institutions with city schools populated by high numbers of students of color and suburban schools populated by a majority of white students.[16] In his many visits to urban schools throughout the country, Kozol writes: "I simply never see white children"[17] and "Virtually all the children of black and Hispanic people in the cities that I visited both large and small, were now attending schools in which their isolation was as absolute as it had been for children in the school in which I'd started so many years before."[18]

These startling findings, in tandem with data about the teaching force, point to a wide discrepancy between the teachers and the urban students they serve. This condition, however, does not imply that White teachers can only teach White students and Black teachers can only teach Black students. Nevertheless, the fact remained that we, the faculty at WGS, were of the same color and class as those who hold the power in American society. It is hard to know how these differences influenced the quality of our relationships with the students. Inevitably, however, differences in race and class probably created initial roadblocks in establishing trust with our students.

> October 20: *It is nearing the end of October and we are just beginning to see the benefits of building trusting relationships with our students. There are so many lessons yet to be learned. Anyone who says, "those who can't do— teach," has never stepped into a classroom and watched the deluge of details that a teacher must handle, even in a time as short as five minutes. Triple this number in the urban classroom and one begins to get a sense of the magnitude of decisions that urban teachers make every day.*

First-year urban teachers are likely to face a shocking incongruity between their expectations of teaching and what the teaching situation actually presents, especially if they haven't had a large degree of hands-on experience and direct discussions about urban children.[19] Although teacher education classes can help pre-service teachers practice the craft of teaching, they cannot replicate the context in which school teaching takes place. For instance, in the space of a few minutes a teacher may experience several students responding at the same time, rapid-fire student questions, facial expressions or body language that may be perceived as supportive or unsupportive, or loud disturbances over issues that happened outside of the classroom. Such demands require lightning-quick decisions and the instantaneous ability to prioritize whose needs to serve.

For that reason, pre-service teachers need both rigorous hands-on experiences and a university learning community that encourages in-depth reflection on those experiences. It is important to note that these experiences work only as well as the fieldwork is meaningful and the reflective discussion is closely aligned with relevant pedagogical theory. The quality of a teacher education program depends on its ability to blend reflection with authentic practice. This is imperative for preparing teachers to teach in urban schools.

How, then, do we prepare pre-service teachers to accept and integrate ideas about the value of trust, culturally responsive teaching, and learning communities? We start by realizing that teachers can't teach something that they don't know. If beginning teachers have not experienced authentic learning communities where cultural sensitivity is a part of the learning process, they can hardly be expected to model these concepts in their own classroom. Participation in a learning group is the kind of learning that must be experienced. While one can enhance this experience with relevant readings, articles cannot substitute for the understanding that comes from working through the process of establishing a learning community.

Learning communities teach pre-service teachers more than cooperation and collaboration. Within the learning community, "future teachers need to learn how to conduct discussions . . . and they must learn to develop situations in which students learn to be willing to test their ideas with their classmates."[20] As such, one would expect to find a learning community where students take ownership of their own learning through problem solving, discussion, individual or group projects, and portfolio assessment techniques. All of these strategies must be modeled so that pre-service teachers can begin to expand their concept of democratic practice.

Educational literature supports three assumptions about teaching/learning. First, students function best in an environment of trust and respect. Second, learning communities are powerful agents in creating a climate for learning. Third, responsiveness to the student's cultural context strengthens relationships between student and teacher. These strands are interwoven and vital to the forward motion of democratic practice.

Not all people, however, are willing to accept these assumptions. To those teachers or administrators who rely on strict control of every facet in the classroom, a community of learning may seem like a ridiculous, ineffective way to teach or run a school. This may have serious ramifications for the democratically minded teacher. When administrators question the merit of democratic teaching practice, teacher evaluations often suffer. Parents, who were schooled in teacher-directed classrooms, may create additional pressure through complaints that the teacher isn't doing his/her job. Whether bureaucratic, community-based, or parental, politics are always part of the equation in the public school system. This makes the move toward democratic practice all the more difficult.

> *October 8: Yesterday was troubling. I stumbled upon some information that foreshadowed major difficulties for the future of our school. By way of a casual conversation over lunch, I learned that each member of the faculty had been individually "summoned" to the head teacher's office for a meeting with the coordinating principal of all academy schools in the district.*
>
> *Each teacher was severely criticized for his/her teaching style or classroom management, and basically told to shape up. Teachers were not treated as professionals nor respected for what that they had accomplished in past month. During the meeting, the head teacher and coordinating principal undermined the university-district partnership with comments like "the university doesn't know how to handle urban education," and "We have been in the business for years and have the experience to deal with these kids."*

"These kids," however tough or vulnerable, deserve teachers who not only care about their well-being but work tirelessly to provide the conditions for authentic learning. One could also generalize that a communal form of learning is far more inclusive than traditional instruction. Sitting immobilized behind a desk while passively listening to lectures day after day may work for some students. But, most of us believed that engaged learning, the kind of learning that persuaded students to reflect on their work in terms of life beyond the classroom, met the needs of many different learning styles. According to hooks, "Seeing the classroom always as a communal place enhances the likelihood of collective effort in creating and sustaining a learning community."[21]

So, why persist with a model of democratic schooling that feels initially uncomfortable and takes time and creative energy to make it work, often against great odds? In terms of the classroom, a teacher persists because a community of inquiry is not only a precious, powerful structure for social and academic learning but also a foundation of democratic practice. In terms of the school, a democratic culture provides a way for students and teachers to continually evaluate the effectiveness of curriculum and policies that affect the care of students and the strength of their learning community.

New teachers should know that building a community of learners rarely progresses smoothly. Instead of a gentle coming together of hearts and minds, the beginnings often involve confusion, discomfort, and lack of cohesion. "Establishing trust," comments Haberman, "may take up to a half of a year in some urban settings. For many students whose lives are confounded with issues of identity, poverty, and lack of social skills, this process may take even longer."[22]

The hundreds of interactions that teachers encounter on a day-to-day basis can divert their attention from the big picture. "Jorge didn't do his homework again." "Molly cries every day." "How can I find a better way to teach algebra so that students see some connections to their lives?" At some point, however, teachers need to reflect on the larger questions that help validate the purpose in their work: "How are we doing in terms of coming together as a community of supportive learners?" "How do we know that we are making headway with the democratic goals that we have established for our classroom/school?" Or, "When do we reach a point at which the school or classroom functions as a democratic unit?"

Because democracy is ever-evolving, there is no "there, there." However, there are guideposts along the way that serve as markers of growth. These markers are couched as a series of questions for contemplation: "Are students free to contribute to the class life through thoughtful ideas or arguments based on valid claims?" "Are teachers free to plan and execute ideas that affect the workings of the school?" "Are school administrators free to guide the school based on a democratic mission?" "Are parents free to collaborate with school personnel in meaningful decisions that impact the school?"

These questions define, in part, a school/classroom characterized as a democratic community of learners. They help to ground our daily work and differentiate between "playing" school (going through the motions of schooling) and building a community that embraces authentic learning to its fullest. Although American society continues to move toward test scores as the measure of success, a learning community aims toward higher goals. Ravitch states, "The schools will surely be failures if students graduate knowing how to choose the right option from four bubbles on a multiple choice test but unprepared to lead fulfilling lives, to be responsible citizens, and to make good choices for themselves, their families, and our society."[23]

The presence of democratic practice, in meeting these goals, nourishes teachers as well as students. Patience with the process is probably the most difficult part of teaching students to work together and respect different points of view. For those who wonder whether democratic learning communities are worth the trouble, it may help to know that the gigantic task of shaping an informed, participatory citizenry happens one lesson at a time, one day at a time, and one year at a time.

NOTES

1. bell hooks, *Teaching to Transgress: Education as the Practice of Freedom* (New York: Routledge, 1994), 8.

2. Patricia B. Kopetz, Anthony J. Lease, and Bonnie Z. Warren-Kring, *Comprehensive Urban Education* (Boston: Pearson, 2006), 199–200.

3. See, for example, Ana Maria Villegas and Tamara Lucas, *Educating Culturally Responsive Teachers: A Coherent Approach* (New York: State University of New York Press, 2002); Dave F. Brown, "Urban Teachers' Professed Classroom Management Strategies: Reflections of Culturally Responsive Teaching," *Urban Education* 39 (2004): 266–289. doi: 10.1177/0042085904263258.

4. Catherine D. Ennis and M. Terri McCauley, "Creating Urban Classroom Communities Worthy of Trust," *Journal of Curriculum Studies* 34, no. 2 (2002): 151. doi: 10.1080/00220270110096370.

5. Deborah Meier, *In Schools We Trust: Creating Communities of Learning in an Era of Testing and Standardization* (Boston: Beacon Press, 2002).

6. Ennis and McCauley, "Creating Urban Classsroom Communities."

7. Ennis and McCauley, "Creating Urban Classsroom Communities," 152.

8. Ennis and McCauley, "Creating Urban Classsroom Communities," 164.

9. Gloria Ladson-Billings, *Crossing Over to Canaan: The Journey of New Teachers in Diverse Classrooms* (San Francisco: Jossey-Bass, 2001), 99.

10. Gloria Ladson-Billings, *The Dreamkeepers: Successful Teachers of African American Children* (San Francisco: Jossey-Bass, 1994), 25.

11. Jean Anyon, "Putting Education at the Center," in *City Kids, City Schools: More Reports from the Front Row,* ed. William Ayers, Gloria Ladson-Billings, Gregory Michie, and Pedro A. Noguera (New York: The New Press, 2008), 313.

12. See, for example, Ana Maria Villegas and Tamara Lucas, *Educating Culturally Responsive Teachers* (New York: State University of New York Press, 2002); Sue Brooks, "What Teachers Need to Know about Poverty," in *Teaching City Kids: Understanding and Appreciating Them,* ed. Joe L. Kincheloe and kecia hayes (New York: Peter Lang, 2007).

13. Jeanne Theoharis, "I Hate It When People Treat Me Like a Fxxx-up," in *Our Schools Suck: Students Talk Back to a Segregated Nation on the Failures of Urban Education,* ed. Gaston Alonso, Noel S. Anderson, Celina Su, and Jeanne Theoharis (New York: New York University Press, 2009), 95.

14. Jessica T. Shiller, "These Are Our Children!: An Examination of Relationship-Building Practices in Urban High Schools," in *Urban Review* 41 (2009): 461–485. doi: 001:10.1007/s11256-008-0110-1.

15. Deborah Meier, *The Power of Their Ideas: Lessons for America from a Small School in Harlem* (Boston: Beacon, 1995), 56.

16. See, for example, Jonathan Kozol, *The Shame of the Nation* (New York: Three Rivers Press, 2005); Gaston Alonso, Noel S. Anderson, Celina Su, and Jeanne Theoharis, *Our Schools Suck: Students Talk Back to a Segregated Nation on the Failures of Urban Education* (New York: New York University Press, 2009).

17. Kozol, *Shame of the Nation,* 10.

18. Kozol, *Shame of the Nation,* 8.

19. Melba Venison, "Effective Teacher Training Programs for Urban School Teachers," in *Best Practices for Teaching Students in Urban Schools,* ed. Rose M. Duhon-Sells, Magellan Studies in Education, vol. 100 (Lewistown, NY: The Edwin Mellen Press, 2004).

20. Nicholas M. Michelli, "Education for Democracy: What Can It Be?" in *Teacher Education for Democracy and Social Justice,* ed. Nicholas M. Michelli and David Lee Keiser (New York: Routledge, 2005), 16.

21. bell hooks, *Teaching to Transgress,* 8.

22. Martin Haberman, *Star Teachers of Children in Poverty* (West Lafayette, IN: Kappa Delta Pi, 1995), 32.

23. Diane Ravitch, *The Death and Life of the Great American School System: How Testing and Choice Are Undermining Education* (New York: Basic Books, 2010), 224.

Chapter Four

They Danced While We Looked Away

Commercial depictions of teachers and students tell us a lot about how others perceive life in the classroom. Among the education magazines or typical book jacket, one usually sees well-dressed students smiling and eagerly waving their hand to answer a question with energetic teachers ready to make magic happen. Such images portray for many what it means to be a teacher. Such images fill the minds of applicants who enter a program of study in teacher education.

A picture, however, is only a snapshot in time. It cannot capture the art of the interaction or the time-intensive process of helping a student learn something new. In fact much about teaching is attending to basic needs for care and belonging. "Before I stepped into my first classroom, I thought teaching was mainly instruction."[1] Experienced teachers know that teaching is multi-dimensional and that instruction is but a part of that kaleidoscopic landscape.

The frenetic pace of urban teaching, from dealing with a child who has just been evicted from her home to prioritizing who, of the ten anxious loud students, has the most pressing question, exemplifies what urban teachers face daily. While some teachers never learn to manage this unrelenting neediness, the most successful teachers are able to troubleshoot while also providing a rich learning-centered experience. These teachers reflect a caring ethic at its best.

To care for students, teachers must not only recognize their individual academic needs but also their emotional needs. Looking back, I realized that the WGS students had engaged me in a dance. It was a dance to see who will give up on whom first. Would I, the teacher, determine that these students are unteachable and, therefore, walk away? Or would the students determine that they are unteachable and walk away from me?

This reminds me of the delicate but enchanting dance of the crane during the mating process. To attract a particular female, the male will plume his feathers and hop in a floating manner from one foot to the other. The male presents different "sides" of himself to the female as if to say, "This is who I am. Take me as I am." My students' dance said, "This is who I am. You could not possibly like me or teach me."

> October 13: *About the middle of October, a new student, Marisol, joined our school. I first met her in music class where she immediately introduced herself and wanted to know about me. At first I was thrilled with this personable teen until I began to see a familiar pattern of interrupting dialogue and calling out no matter what the question. At one point she interrupted me . . . "Hey, Dr. D. You have bowed legs" (I did). All the kids stared at my legs while Marisol seemed pleased to have noticed something that the others had not. In other words, the emotional content of the statement and its effect on me did not cross her mind. She was just happy to have noticed something before someone else did.*

Little by little I began to learn about Marisol. She let me know that her brother had been murdered and that she grieved terribly for him. Her mother entertained men at night so Marisol was left to hold the house together. She was only fifteen years old, a vulnerable child herself, aching for some trace of stability. She would give me a big hug, then seconds later, scream obscenities at another student for some transgression. She could just as well explode at me if I needed to be firm with her. Marisol's rage was fierce, yet she openly craved affection and affirmation.

Marisol's story was not unlike many in the class. The majority of students came from backgrounds, which, as Sato and Lensmire suggest, "lie far outside the realm of most teachers' experience."[2] Urban classrooms are filled with students, many of whom have lives characterized by the following aspects: born to unmarried parents, are a year or more behind in school, were born poor or are poor, are living in a family receiving food stamps, live with parents without health insurance, live with a relative, or speak a language at home other than English, and so on.[3]

A lot of information about my students' lives came from the guidance counselor and other school personnel. I learned that we had to be cautious dealing with John's dad because in his anger, he would take away visiting rights with John's mother. I learned that Tanya had been writing graphic poems about sexual abuse. I learned that Jorge's mother had died last year and that he was in a deep depression. I learned that Brandon was homeless and living in a shelter. He had been separated from his brother and spent much of his time wondering how to find him. Another student, Maria, was angry and ill tempered most of the time. Eventually we learned that her mother had given her to an aunt, where she was unwanted, while the mother left for an undetermined stay in Colombia with her boyfriend.

I was taken aback by the amount of physical thumb-sucking among the girls. Not only did they openly and shamelessly suck their thumbs during class but also the rest of the students seemed to tacitly accept this behavior as the normal course of things. Some of the stressors originated at home where students were often put in the position of parenting their own parent(s) and assuming adult roles in the family. Other stressors originated outside of the home in terms of unhealthy relationships with peers or street survival behavior. Not surprisingly, some of our students were tormented to join gangs. There was an ongoing undercurrent of whispering about the Crips and the Bloods, two dangerous and nationally established street gangs.

One day LaToya walked slowly and arthritically into school. Her face was a mass of swollen bruises that made her speech strained and labored. At the time, I thought, "child abuse," but now believe that she had undergone a brutal initiation for entry into a gang. There were rarely any uplifting stories. Each child had a heartbreaking story and each child's story offered vivid information about his/her school behavior.

Although one could easily use these stories to excuse delinquent behavior, the fact is that classroom settings must maintain a sense of peace and safety for learning to take place. How, then, does one care for students who often behave in ways that are unlovable not only to the teacher or those around them, but more tragically to themselves as well? Despite their personal circumstances, it is hard to care about students who say hurtful things to their peers. It is hard to care about students who stand up and yell across the room during a lesson even though their life experience may reinforce that kind of behavior.

While it is difficult to care for students that give us a hard time, it is important to remember that the teacher can become the bridge from students' unbearable conditions to bearable lives. There are no magic bullets for dealing with students who hurt but we have a tenable obligation to give care in the form of empathy, high standards, and reasonable expectations. How we prepare pre-service teachers for such a challenge depends on our own in-depth understanding of the social and emotional lives of urban children and our ability to sensitively communicate this in a pedagogical context.

Educating children of poverty, where students are neglected or exposed to bitter turbulence on a daily basis, presents complex issues. Urban students, especially in high school, have accumulated thick layers of distrust and anger.[4] This, in addition to the residue from typical adolescence behavior, often ignites what might be very commonplace events in another setting.

Although urban youth come to school with what seem like insurmountable problems, teachers cannot lose hope in reaching their students. In one sense, the school plays an essential role as a "secondary caregiver."[5] Kopetz and her colleagues theorize that while children do undergo deep stress, the strength of their coping mechanisms generates the resilience to rebound.[6]

The problem arises when the stressors outweigh the child's capacity for resilience. Here the school can help the student strengthen or gain additional coping mechanisms. While we tend to think about the school in terms of cognitive activities such as specific content, textbooks, and tests, teaching children to manage their emotional lives serves a critical purpose as well.[7] "We need to remember that academics and social behavior are profoundly intertwined."[8]

Nel Noddings,[9] one of the front-runners in advocating care as an indispensible disposition of teaching, cautions that care is not synonymous with love and good urban teachers know not to confuse the two. Caring is more than a hug or a compliment. Rather, authentic caring is an ongoing interactive process of helping children to succeed in life.

Good teachers show caring best when they help their students develop independence and the capacity to problem solve both cognitive and emotional issues. Teachers show caring in the language they use to communicate both pleasure and displeasure with students. Teachers also show caring when they provide a classroom that engages students with others to actively construct knowledge.

In an interesting study on urban classroom management, Brown studied how teachers managed classroom practice and relationships with students.[10] His study included extensive interviews with teachers from first through twelfth grade classrooms in urban schools within seven American cities. The findings, in line with other literature on urban education,[11] posit that good urban teachers reflect the following five traits:

1. They have strong personal relationships with their students.
2. They build a caring learning environment that lends itself to a democratic community.
3. They maintain a business-like classroom.
4. They engage in congruent communication.
5. They demonstrate assertiveness and clear expectations.

Whereas one might expect these characteristics in all good teachers, they are especially powerful with students who often come from unstructured and economically deprived circumstances.

Caring in teaching means many things besides the relationship between teacher and student. Other evidences of care are reflected in the type of content chosen for study, the cultural responsiveness to learning, and the determination to maintain high expectations. Delpit and others have stressed the need for firm discipline, particularly with African American children. Although outsiders may misconstrue this behavior as mean or too "pushy," according to Delpit, parents in the African American community expect an authority figure commensurate with assertive, demanding behavior. [12]

She states, "In many African American communities, teachers are expected to show that they care about their students by controlling the class, exhibiting personal power; establishing meaningful interpersonal relationships; displaying emotion to garner student respect; and demonstrating the belief that all students can learn."[13] Further, "Teachers who do not exhibit these behaviors may be viewed by community members as ineffectual, boring, or uncaring."[14]

Some might think that this contradicts the profile of a teacher engaged in democratic practice where conditions support questioning, problem solving, and student-centered learning. On the contrary, Delpit is not suggesting a particular teaching approach but rather that Black students look to the teacher to maintain a sense of fairness and trust. One need not misinterpret control as oppressive. Such dispositions can also suggest a caring teacher who brings both structure and care to children who desperately need stability in their lives. "'Fussing behavior' is not a mean-spirited attempt to harm students. It is the caring, yet authoritarian explicit explanation that says, 'I expect more from you.'"[15]

Themes of care and caring are painfully absent in our teaching discourse and our teacher training.[16] We tend to focus instruction on intellectual development rather than the affective dimensions that influence purposeful learning. Real caring is not easy nor is it always a natural extension of teaching. How to prepare novice teachers for this elusive disposition and its pedagogical realization lies squarely in the lap of the teacher education program.

First-year teachers, for instance, are especially amazed at the lack of social and emotional skills in their students.[17] This suggests that teacher educators not only provide experiences to learn about an ethic of caring in the classroom but also *how to teach* their own students to care and to respect each other. Teaching students to care is not part of the typical education program, yet without some direct instruction the art of caring remains at the teacher level rather than a part of the education of students.

Teachers must learn that all substantive relationships go through periods of unrest, homeostasis, and positive growth. Novice teachers should grow to expect disagreement, quarrels, and discontent as a normal outgrowth of people learning to get along with other people. Given this, they also need strategies for handling the negative forces that fracture rather than bond a class of students.

As the "practice of freedom," education can and should serve a liberating role.[18] Teaching, at its best, ought to initiate a transformative process that seeks to empower students for successful life within society rather than foster dependency and victimization. Teaching for critical thinking and thoughtfulness in both emotional and academic areas contributes to the student's feeling of capability. This lends itself to a healthy and caring democratic environment.

While peer relationships may seem to take priority in adolescence, this should not undermine the importance of the adult in the adolescent's life.[19] Friends can provide emotional support, but an adult brings maturity and wisdom to the relationship. Research also indicates that students are more likely to work harder for a significant adult than one who has little importance in the student's life.[20] As indicated in earlier chapters, trust remains the key element in forging a positive, caring bond between teacher and student.

In my teaching at WGS, I assumed that students merely tolerated adults and had no intention of wanting to know anything more than the cars we drove to school. I knew the power of peer friendships at this age and mistakenly concluded that students would never accept more than a surface-level relationship with me (something that proved wrong the longer I taught). Yet, the natural, raw beauty of these children, protected behind a guise of acerbic language and inappropriate behavior, sometimes glimmered regardless:

> October 20: *I have seen vestiges of the goodness in my students during moments when they were often unaware. Their tough street façade may take center stage, as if they have to protect the human core at all cost, yet not one of my students seems threatening or physically violent. While the behavior is often bewildering, I am not afraid of these children. Even in Shariff's wildest moments, he is more like a little boy crying for help than a menacing eighteen-year-old.*

For those of us coming from a life of privilege where schooling was the centerpiece of our world, the students' personal stories were well beyond anything that we had experienced. Sometimes one wonders whether students should be congratulated just for coming to school, let alone completing any work. Kincheloe comments that "the traumatic events students may have suffered at home, on the way to school, or at school in the bathroom or other places hidden from public view, may make it extremely difficult for [students] to concentrate on the lesson *du jour*."[21] In seeing troubled and hungry students every day, were rigorous academic standards were even possible?

According to the literature on urban education the most successful urban teachers ardently believe quite the opposite; you are failing your students if you do not expect high standards despite the problems that they experience outside of school. "The only way that I think you can eradicate poverty," said Mrs. Willis, "is to educate them."[22] Teaching urban children demands persistence grounded in the belief that urban children can and will learn. Commenting on pre-service education, Ladson-Billings remarks, "We have to do a better job of seeing past the students' missionary zeal to 'help those poor children.'"[23]

This belief could not be more indicative of Robbin's teaching, a wonderful teacher and friend, who grew up and continues to live in the inner city where she teaches. In her town, most of the families live below the poverty line. She often reminds my pre-service college students that while they may feel sadness about students' situations, they cannot allow that sadness to interfere with having high standards.

"You don't help these kids by feeling sorry for them," she says passionately. "These students have got to learn how to live in our society, however flawed and discriminatory it may be. If you want them to succeed, they have to learn the language of success and what it takes to succeed in today's society." Robbin is not calloused to her student's pain. On the contrary, she cares deeply for these students and demands a level of respect and responsibility that she believes will carry them through life. She would be the first to say that "teaching is a matter of love"[24] and her students reflect that trust daily.

Robbin is a prototype of what Ware calls a "warm demander": one who approaches learning from the standpoint that teaching is not content-based but contextually driven.[25] The student's style of discourse, cultural identity, and special learning needs form a unique but comprehensive portrait of the student. Warm demanders are highly successful in reaching urban students and helping them learn. As a warm demander, Robbin may run her classroom in a tough love fashion but she also recognizes and responds to individual students' needs. An empathic listener, she is the one teacher to whom students come when feeling troubled or needing reassurance. She builds strong relationships with the parents or caregivers who may, in fact, be "children" themselves. In her wisdom, she understands the insight that parents/caregivers and the community bring to the educational setting.

At WGS we were certainly "warm" but not demanding in the way that tells students, "We expect a lot from you." Most troubling, our teaching style was out of sync with the rest of our students' worlds. Although some of the literature suggests that urban children initially have most comfort with a direct, authoritarian style of teaching, our style of teaching was more indirect. These different styles of teaching do not mean that urban children cannot learn or greatly benefit from a different teaching approach. It suggests, however, that knowing the students' comfort level might have informed us to proceed with more caution. Given the new school, a primarily white faculty, and ambiguity in school procedures, our constructivist teaching approach must have contributed significantly to the students' anxiety and need for control.

October 31: *At the end of October, the students were invited to plan a Hallo-ween party. Marisol was as engaged as the others in planning the food, activ-ities, etc. I looked forward to the party as it was one of the first social events at the school and I hoped to see a different side of my students. I was right—I did see a different side of my students, never anticipating which side I was about to see.*

When I arrived the party was already in progress, Marisol came running up to me and started undulating her body in front of me. My unschooled reaction was to play along while attempting to comically show a more appro-priate dance move. Yes, that's right, the kids were all watching and howling. I realized my mistaken perception when she pushed her rear into me and started moving in a circular motion. I felt trapped and embarrassed.

For the rest of the evening, I watched Marisol as she interacted with the other students. She had a strange way of unloading huge amounts of affection and then the next minute tuning out her friends as if they never existed. I felt such sadness as I watched this young girl. She was dancing what she knew— things that a young girl should never have to know.

Many of the other girls were dancing in a similar way but not as sugges-tively. Tyrone, however, was right in the thick of things. He and another girl started to dance close to the floor. The students must have known that this was pushing the limits because they tightly formed a circle and tried to keep the dancers out of adult vision.

Not wanting to watch the action in the middle of the dance floor, the faculty who attended the event pretended to be absorbed in other things. Questions raced through my head: Should I stop the inappropriate dancing? Are my values outdated? How do kids learn to limit their behavior if adults are policing them all the time? Do I have a right to address this at all? Do I have the courage to spoil their fun?

In hindsight I realize that I should have intervened . . . that some of the other students were uncomfortable and looked to adults to set limits. As the evening continued, we, the faculty, fell into a stunned stupor when things seemed to spiral out of control. The students danced while we looked away. Rules for governing dance behavior would never have occurred to us—what we saw that night was completely out of the realm of our imagination. None of us had experience with teens from this era. None of us watched MTV. The students were having a great time! We wanted to crawl under a rock. The students finally had a sense of pride in their school. We didn't like their idea of a school. If ever we perceived a gap between our lives and our students' lives, the Halloween party assured us that we were staring in the face of the Grand Canyon.

This boldly illustrates a clash of cultures between the faculty and the students. But to which culture should we respond? The culture of adoles-cence? The culture of race? The culture of poverty? This dilemma under-scores the complexity of working with adolescents and raises our consciousness to the contextual puzzles that occur when dealing with human beings. Whether the dancing was a reflection of the students' culture or what they gleaned from TV only scratches the surface of larger questions: Did such dancing provide an avenue for harmless fun or was it a reflection of students' lack of respect for themselves as well as the other students who would not participate?

Here's the problem: These are the wrong questions! The difficulty in addressing these questions lies in the ambiguity of the term "moral," which I believe kept the faculty from taking some action. Most people initially connect "moral" or "morality" with a "good-bad" continuum anchored in a religious context. For that reason, none of us wanted to project moral judgment on the dancing. Any hint of moral judgment smacked in the face of building honest and trusting relationships, or so we thought.

Another way to interpret moral, however, has to do with honorable or just actions as in a "moral obligation." Teachers, for instance, have a moral obligation when it comes to upholding the rights of the student/students. It is a problem of moral consequence when anything advantages some students over others. The lack of resources in urban schools when compared to suburban schools, for example, provides a stark reminder of the urban inequities that students face. These inequities such as access to technology, well-equipped science labs, and spacious libraries with up-to-date holdings casts a disturbing light on what some students have as a normal part of their school day while others do not.

Teachers deal with issues of moral consequence every day, simply because any decision that concerns human beings involves a moral component.[26] In this sense, relationships with students, decisions about curriculum, and equality in instruction all involve a moral dimension. Although the moral dimensions of teaching are often misunderstood, they undergird our commitment to providing a safe learning environment where students have resources for enhancing learning, a classroom environment that honors each student's contributions, and knowledgeable, caring teachers.

In terms of the Halloween party, our first reactions centered on our discomfort with judgments based on a traditional usage of moral values—that is, a personal value system about what is good behavior and what is not. Had we reframed our question in terms of how students learn to sustain a community of people who have respect for all of us, we probably would have intervened immediately. From a democratic perspective, the problem was not about social morality but whether adolescents were building a community in which all had a valuable part. Teaching for democratic practice, then, shifts from issues of "good girl, bad boy" to questions about why such behavior might be viewed as oppressive to both the individual and the group.

Anything that prevents students from coexisting in a peaceful, supportive environment diminishes the rights of students to authentically participate. In terms of the democratic process, respect for others, and more importantly for one's self is a key attribute of forming a democratically based classroom. It leads to the assurance that one's contributions as well as those of others are valid and worthwhile. Thus, a caring school environment has the potential (and moral obligation) for promoting stability and creating a sense of belonging for marginalized students.[27]

Nicholas Michelli, in his chapter "Education for Democracy: What Can It Be?," puts forth salient questions about teachers' responsibilities for the civic behavior of their students. He writes:

> One of the broader ways to think about education for democracy is to consider the "civil" responsibilities of individuals. What does it mean to be civil as a participant in a democratic society? How does one deal with disagreements and resolve them? How might we treat other persons we encounter, especially when their beliefs and views are different from our own? What are the implications for flexibility and empathy in dealing with other perspectives? How do we examine and engender respect for others in the way we deal with differing positions? If these are qualities of a democratic life . . . then the responsibility goes beyond the social studies teacher and becomes the responsibility of all teachers. Learning to be respectful does not mean accepting all positions put forth as equally valid.[28]

Michelli points to a critical issue: That civil behavior does and must involve a level of respect for others. To this I add that respect refers not only to ideas but principled, thoughtful behavior as well. For it stands to reason that civic responsibilities involve more than self-interest. Consequently, teaching for democratic practice demands that we engage students in continual discussion about the tension between the individual freedom and freedom for the common good.

In schools, we probably don't spend enough time thinking about behavior in terms of freedom and how students' behavior can suppress or support the freedom of others. Questions about what is best for the student also undergird teacher decision making. For example, should teachers choose to give a higher grade based on a low-functioning student's tremendous individual progress or use a standardized scoring system for everyone? Should a music teacher include an enthusiastic student with poor musical skills in an ensemble even if it diminishes the quality of the group? In other words, opportunities for democratic participation often occur not in "glossy political rhetoric, but in the details of everyday lives."[29]

Essentially, it takes courage, from a caring foundation, to take a stand in the face of possible student discontent or faculty disapproval. When to proceed cautiously and when to proceed with forthright conviction is not always clear. This lack of clarity characterizes why teaching remains so difficult and why fixed rules of how to teach are so absurd. Much of democratic practice depends not only on the teacher's deep knowledge of the student but strong instincts as well. For exemplary teachers, this is just common sense.

NOTES

1. William Ayers, *To Teach: The Journey of a Teacher,* 2nd ed. (New York: Teachers College Press, 2001), 4.
2. Mistlina Sato and Timothy J. Lensmire, "Poverty and Payne: Supporting Teachers to Work with Children of Poverty," *Phi Delta Kappan* 90, no. 5 (2009): 365.
3. Patricia B. Kopetz, Anthony J. Lease, and Bonnie Z. Warren-Kring, *Comprehensive Urban Education* (Boston: Pearson, 2006), 70–71.
4. Catherine D. Ennis and M. Terri McCauley, "Creating Urban Classroom Communities Worthy of Trust," *Journal of Curriculum Studies* 34, no. 2 (2002): 149–172. doi: 10.1080/0022027011009637O.
5. Kopetz, et al., *Comprehensive Urban Education,* 70–71.
6. Kopetz, et al., *Comprehensive Urban Education,* 70–71.
7. Melba Venison, "Effective Teacher Training Programs for Urban School Teachers," in *Best Practices for Teaching Students in Urban Schools,* ed. Rose M. Duhon-Sells, Magellan Studies in Education, vol. 100 (Lewistown, NY: The Edwin Mellen Press, 2004).
8. Ruth Sidney Charney, *Teaching Children to Care: Management in the Responsive Classroom* (Greenfield, MA: Northeast Foundation for Children, 1992), 11.
9. Nel Noddings, *The Challenge to Care in Schools,* 2nd ed. (New York: Teachers College Press, 2005).
10. Dave F. Brown, "Urban Teachers' Professed Classroom Management Strategies: Reflections of Culturally Responsive Teaching," *Urban Education* 39 (2004): 266–289. doi: 10.1177/0042085904263258.
11. See, for example, Ruben Garza, "Latino and White High School Students' Perception of Caring Behaviors: Are We Culturally Responsive to Our Students?" *Urban Education* 44 (2009): 297–321. doi: 10.1177/0042085908318714; Jessica T. Shiller, "These Are Our Children!: An Examination of Relationship-Building Practices in Urban High Schools," *Urban Review* 41 (2009): 461–485. doi: 001:10.1007/s11256-008-0110-1; Marguerite Vanden Wyngaard, "Culturally Responsive Pedagogies," in *Teaching City Kids: Understanding and Appreciating Them,* ed. Joe L. Kincheloe and kecia hayes (New York: Peter Lang, 2007), 121–130.
12. Lisa Delpit, *Other People's Children* (New York: The New Press, 2006), 142.
13. Delpit, *Other People's Children,* 142.
14. Delpit, *Other People's Children,* 142.
15. Franita Ware, "Warm Demander Pedagogy: Culturally Responsive Teaching That Supports a Culture of Achievement for African American Students," *Urban Education* 41, no. 4 (2006): 452. doi: 10.1177/0042085906289710.
16. Nel Noddings, "Teaching Themes of Care," *Phi Delta Kappan* 76, no. 9 (1995): 675–679.
17. Venison, "Effective Teacher Training Programs," 42.
18. Paulo Freire, *Pedagogy of the Oppressed,* trans. Myra Bergman Ramos (New York: Continuum, 1990).
19. Deborah Meier, *In Schools We Trust: Creating Communities of Learning in an Era of Testing and Standardization* (Boston: Beacon, 2002).
20. Ennis and McCauley, "Creating Urban Classroom Communities," 164.
21. Joe L. Kincheloe, "City Kids—Not The Kind of Students You'd Want to Teach," in *Teaching City Kids: Understanding and Appreciating Them,* ed. Joe L. Kincheloe and kecia hayes (New York: Peter Lang, 2007), 15.

22. Ware, "Warm Demander Pedagogy," 443–444. Mrs. Willis was a participant in Ware's research study.

23. Gloria Ladson-Billings, *Crossing Over to Canaan: The Journey of New Teachers in Diverse Classrooms* (San Francisco: Jossey–Bass, 2001), 126.

24. Ayers, *To Teach: The Journey of a Teacher*, 18.

25. Ware, "Warm Demander Pedagogy."

26. John I. Goodlad, "The Occupation of Teaching in Schools," in *The Moral Dimensions of Teaching,* ed. John I. Goodlad, Roger Soder, and Kenneth A. Sirotnik (San Francisco: Jossey-Bass, 1991), 30.

27. Noddings, *The Challenge to Care*, 25.

28. Nicholas M. Michelli, "Education for Democracy: What Can It Be?" in *Teacher Education for Democracy and Social Justice,* ed. Nicholas M. Michelli and David Lee Keiser (New York: Routledge, (2005), 5.

29. Michael W. Apple and James A. Beane, "Lessons from Democratic Schools," in *Democratic Schools,* ed. Michael W. Apple and James A. Beane (Alexandria, VA: Association for Supervision and Curriculum Development, 1995), 103.

Chapter Five

Teachable Moments, Part 1

Teachers rarely forget that moment when a simple comment or change in direction created a whole new set of possibilities for student learning. When teachers refer to a "teachable moment" they often mean a fortuitous moment in a lesson that opens the door for some real learning to take place. It is an "aha" moment for both the student and the teacher.

These teachable moments occur, not in prescriptive, clear-cut solutions, but rather in messy, often stress-provoked incidences that summon the teacher's most insightful gifts for translating social or academic dilemmas into life lessons. When both students and teachers reach common ground in the midst of emotionally laced problems, the experience has a powerful impact on all.

> November 16: *Today was supposed to be a big deal for my students and myself. We had put together a musical program tracing the development of Rhythm and Blues from the 1950s to the present. Presentations ranged from choreographed dances to spoken narratives about the social scene to technological advances in recording. As the very first school-wide assembly, my students and I felt a jumble of butterflies and nervous excitement that, to me, felt just about right for a before-the-concert situation. By mid-way, the students had already captured the audience's heart judging by the raucous applause and hoots of support.*
>
> *In the final act, my joy turned to astonishment as the dance group (representing music of the present) morphed into an MTV style of dance and costume. Nothing in the presentation reflected the work that they had done in class. (Clearly I didn't learn much from the Halloween party). What's more, instead of using the "clean" version of their song, they used the original recording with lyrics that were not only appalling in terms of degrading women but also included racist lyrics. At a climactic point in the music, they threw off their jackets to reveal skimpy, spaghetti strap shirts that were cut high*

enough to expose a considerable portion of their midriff. Their bawdy gestures articulated the pulsating rapster as students applauded wildly and faculty looked on with cold stares.

Whereas I had every reason to believe that this group would close the program on a positive note, I was stunned with their live performance. Apparently, the group met after school to rework the dance in a way that they believed would enhance the performance. In fact, their revisions created damaging consequences for the entire program. What started out as an endearing portfolio of student work over the past six weeks ended with an exhibition that shocked the adults in the audience.

No amount of explanation would salvage my position. The faculty disdainfully marched past me with a few weak-hearted "thank you for putting this assembly together." I was mortified and embarrassed. As I drove home that afternoon I wondered if it were even possible to turn this fiasco into a poignant lesson for the students.

Erring in public is a teacher's greatest fear, whether through a live performance, exhibition, or publicized test scores. In effect, the damage has to do with community's assumptions that this represents the entire sum of the teacher's work. Moreover, it magnifies the product and diminishes the process that is usually a more telling indicator of student progress. Although it may seem that the music or art teachers are particularly vulnerable to criticism, given the public nature of periodic concerts and displays of student art work, the current emphasis on testing as a measure of teacher effectiveness also involves levels of public scrutiny.

Diane Ravitch, in her best-selling book, *The Death and Life of the Great American School System,* carefully examines the testing frenzy, among many other variables, that affects the success of public schools. Her comment that "standardized tests were not designed to capture the most important dimensions of education" bears significantly on the misperception that a single measure can account for the real advances that students make in the process of learning.[1]

Unfortunately, the public rarely sees when teachers create innovative paths for students to move forward. When criticism of the product overshadows the student's meaningful steps along the way, there is a narrowing of vision about what education means. Consequently, my experience with the assembly program forced me to take a deeper look at the purpose and process leading up to the concert.

Overall, the students had accomplished exactly what I intended for this project. That is, the program demonstrated diverse ways of presenting information and reflected an admirable first step in music research and cross-disciplinary learning. The final dance group—that which caused me the greatest trauma—actually fulfilled their task of presenting music of contemporary society. Although a disturbing portrait, the dancers did use music and dance moves of mainstream pop music—at least from an adolescent's perspective.

My dilemma, then, centered on how to use this episode as a learning experience without lapsing into moral platitudes or warnings about future performances. Questions began to materialize: "Does art lack integrity because it makes us uncomfortable? Should an artist use public taste to frame his/her artwork? Does freedom of speech have limits? What does sexually explicit dancing say about women? What role does the school play in presenting controversial subjects/presentations?"

These questions sparked a cluster of themes including free speech, the rights of women in society, adolescent sexuality, and street culture versus school culture. Ironically, it also brought to the forefront the right of students to make mistakes. For if a democratically based school is a laboratory for civic behavior, how can we teach critical thinking and good judgment without letting students make mistakes? While all of these themes had roots in democratic practice, how to weave these questions into a productive conversation with ninth grade students presented the biggest challenge.

To my surprise the resulting conversation was focused, civil, and intense. The students had no idea that they had done anything but their best work until they began to hear negative comments from the head teacher and other teachers. They actively engaged in discussion:

November 20: *The students were amazingly thoughtful and all wanted a voice in the conversation. Below are excerpts from their discussion about the final dance:*

- *We did exactly what we were supposed to do for the assignment.*
- *Our costumes and gestures were carefully chosen. We did not imitate what we see on TV but only used this as a guide. For instance, we did not think that wearing tight shirts that revealed the outer breast were appropriate. We tried to make costumes with our school audience in mind. Our gestures were not nearly as suggestive as what we see on TV or in our lives.*
- *This type of dancing does not degrade women. We really don't understand what you mean.*
- *Art should reflect life, both the good and the bad.*

I will never forget the passion with which these students argued their point of view while also listening respectfully to others even when they disagreed. The conversation reached well beyond the surface of casual talk and while the conclusions reached were not always in line with my thinking, it didn't matter. The students showed thoughtfulness and empathy in a form I had not seen before. For me, this was truly a teachable moment and an exercise in democracy.

Teachable moments are born from problematic situations that seemingly have no resolution yet rely on the teacher's intuition to find a new path to discovery. Issues with a strong affective component particularly deserve processing, because students who come to the table with strong feelings have a bigger investment in the dialogue. On the other hand, emotionally charged issues carry the risk of inflaming rather than diffusing the situation. The teacher's dilemma of whether to intervene or not is one of those split-second decisions that characterizes the intricacy of dealing with human beings.

There are viable reasons for intervening, not the least of which is the opportunity for students to learn something meaningful about themselves in relation to the greater good. These are the kinds of teachable moments that lead to a feeling of closeness between the teacher and students, having tackled a difficult problem together. Collaborative problem solving, whether accidental or planned, puts teachers and students on an even playing field. This eliminates the need to be "right" and softens the unequal power position that exists between teachers and students.

Emotional closeness also serves a critical role in students' perception of a "good teacher." Wyngaard's study of African American high school students discovered that students' personal relationship with their teachers were linked to students' ideas of what it means to be an adult.[2] Findings indicated that students viewed good teachers as independent and assertive yet always inviting student's opinions, thus giving palpable credence to learning as a team effort. Students also felt that good teachers responded to the students' life stories with dignity and openness.

A nonjudgmental attitude is especially crucial when working with urban adolescents who are often the recipients of harsh societal and family criticism. Moreover, the criticism is generally tinged with moralistic undertones which frame behavior as good or bad. Adolescents are particularly aware of the public's negative perception regarding urban teens. They often brand themselves as "ghetto kids," which in turn, shapes their sense of hopelessness about climbing out of despairing circumstances.

As noted in chapter 3, the importance of adults in students' lives cannot be understated. Responsible adults teach lessons in life that help adolescents grow up. Parents, extended family, pastors, and teachers offer opportunities for students to learn by simply observing how they handle conflicts. In fact, adolescents often lack adult role models in their lives and, unfortunately some of the closest adults do not always model responsible behavior.[3]

Teachers, therefore, play a critical role as adult models for children/adolescents. It is possible, as Haberman suggests, that teachers may be the only models of professionalism with which inner-city children have contact:

Children in poverty are less likely to have out-of-school models who are practicing chemists, language interpreters, writers, or others who can serve as models of knowledgeable people who derive great well-being as lifelong students of various disciplines. I am not referring here merely to occupations and professions (i.e., lawyers, doctors, accountants, etc.) but to the daily experiences of interacting with adults who study and learn because they are well-educated, enthusiastic students of subjects from which they derive personal— not monetary or tangible benefit.[4]

More often than not, adolescents depend on the adults in their lives to broaden their vision and nudge them toward examining issues/events from a different point of view. There are countless opportunities for teachers to challenge the status quo if they have the bravery to do so. For example, in a social studies unit on slavery in the United States, asking whether we can assign levels of seriousness to acts of genocide ("Are acts of slavery different from the Nazi persecution in World War II?") encourages students to examine genocide as an ethical dilemma.

Challenging the status quo, however, requires both critical and responsible thinking. Rarely do life's problems have simple solutions. It is more the case that problems involve many contextual variables that belie clear-cut decisions. Teachers who instruct from a democratic framework realize that students need many opportunities to wrestle with life problems that arise from academic content or adolescent culture. These circumstances encourage students to confront their beliefs and the ramifications of their decisions with regard to perpetuating a good society.

To prepare students for a democratic society, then, we must provide our students with problematic situations that do not lend themselves to immediate resolution. Greene states, "Teachers, like their students, have to learn to love the questions, as they come to realize that there can be no final agreements or answers, no final commensurability."[5] Thinking critically about a situation, teasing out the pros and cons, untangling one's belief system from the evidence at hand all takes place when teachers and students engage in this form of complex problem solving. These are the dispositions that foster critical judgment and thoughtful action, two dispositions essential in a democratic society.

The most challenging problems are often those with a strong emotional component. Issues of social justice involving gender, race, socio-economic status, or persons with disabilities, for instance, provide material for examination in all disciplines as well as contemporary society. Moreover such issues constantly arise in a school environment and are highly tangible to students.

Discussions centered on issues of social justice require a certain amount of courage on the teacher's part. It is uncomfortable to deal with issues of human equity and fairness as they may open the door for pedantic moralizing or dialogue that is insensitive to certain members of the class. For these reasons, some teachers either avoid problems that involve matters of human rights or sidestep the issue by discussing the "outer edges" of the problem. Yet, when the rights of the individual or the group are at the heart of the problem, the teacher has an opportunity to generate many teachable moments. Democratic practice suggests that teachers and students have an obligation to reflect, discuss, and sometimes act on problems that compromise the rights of the individual or group.

Take, for example, a student conversation before or during class in which the word "gay" comes up. In adolescent culture, the term "gay" has become mainstream language. Adolescents sometimes use the term to bully or harass, but more often than not to tease or chide a friend for silly or offbeat behavior: "You are soooo gay." No matter what the situation, students can knowingly or unknowingly hurt those who may be homosexual or have homosexual parents or friends. From a democratic standpoint, this is a situation that pits the right to free speech against the rights of a minority group along with the students' right to have a safe learning space.

If such a situation occurred in the classroom some teachers might immediately stop and say, "That language is inappropriate for our class." Others might choose to ignore the remark because confronting the situation might embarrass certain students. A third alternative is to address it at a later time when the rawness of situation is not so acute. Lastly, the conditions may be such that the teacher might see this opportunity as a teachable moment and address the issue head on. Given the delicate balance of adolescent-teacher relationships, teachers must decide for themselves how to intervene.

All of the above are dependent upon the context: Is this a good time to stop the lesson? Will I embarrass a specific student by addressing the issue? Would it be better to wait until the next session so I have time to think about a positive approach to the problem? Will all students benefit from a discussion on the ramifications of language or should it be handled privately?

Often teachers want to address the remark but do not know how to go about it from a democratic framework. The following scenario presents one way of dealing with hurtful language. A teacher can use his/her content area to talk about the significant contributions of a particular gay person (without acknowledging his/her sexual preference) in that field. After some discussion the teacher might ask, "Does it make any difference if you knew this person was gay?" "Does being gay affect your perception of the individual's contribution?" The teacher must probe further about the use of language and how even terminology that seems innocuous can be painful to others. Because every student in the room has been hurt by some careless or intentional remark, it is not difficult to tap into that feeling as a way of helping students become more empathic.

Discussion based on democratic principles is not to be confused with amateur therapy nor can this book prescribe a discussion process that relates to all classrooms. However, issues that bring democratic principles into contention almost always involve feelingful reactions rooted in a belief system. The charge of the teacher is to redirect students' feeling into conscious awareness of the democratic issue at stake and to help students problem solve actions that preserve the rights of others. Clearly one must proceed cautiously. Any implication of judgment on the part of the teacher compromises the power of the discussion. Further, the teacher must be prepared for callous or thoughtless student responses.

Ultimately the teacher strives to plant seeds of doubt in the student's mind, like a grain of sand in the oyster. Discomfort arises from confronting habits of behavior or deeply held beliefs that impinge on what the student holds as truth. It is hard for both teachers and students to examine their beliefs more closely. Not to engage in messy problem solving, however, risks overlooking the tiny pearl within.

Critical pedagogy, grounded in democratic practice, demands that teachers dare to challenge the thinking and long-held assumptions of themselves and of their students. At its core, critical pedagogy involves an understanding of students not just from an academic perspective but also through familial relationships, standard discourse, distinctive features of the locale, and patterns of how people relate to one another. "Critical urban teachers become explorers of the worlds of their students, their social and cultural contexts as well as the mind spaces produced by operating in such locales."[6]

Many fine teacher education programs encourage students to develop a sense of critical pedagogy as they progress through their curriculum. Attention to critical pedagogy in the urban setting is especially important because pre-service candidates tend to gravitate toward field experiences and teaching positions that mirror their own schooling experience. Some universities, in fact, have designed special programs for students interested in urban teaching. These opportunities open the door for studying critical urban pedagogy and participating in urban field experiences.

Although this book focuses on urban teaching, it is important to remember that urban adolescents can learn a lot from teachers who grew up in suburbia, as can suburban adolescents learn a great deal from working with teachers from the inner city. In both cases, pre-service teachers need academic and field experiences in these different settings to challenge their conceptions of what it means to teach and for whom they teach.

Teaching for democratic practice, while complex and challenging, cannot help but present dilemmas that, when confronted, deepen a student's perspective of the world. Issues of social justice arise from academic content or adolescent culture. "In reality there are 'teachable moments' for social justice everywhere, and a teacher who is primed and committed to noticing and responding to such moments can infuse values of belonging, right treatment, and justice throughout the day."[7]

In a democratically based school, teachers are mindful of student behavior as a starting place for growing up. Good teachers have a long-term vision that recognizes reflection, critical thinking, and conscientious decision making as a cornerstone of fully functioning adults in a democratic society. From this point of view, it is entirely appropriate to stop a lesson in order to process behavior that raises questions about equity, justice, or simple kindness.

So, too, teachers must seek out the problematic within specific disciplines. The ethics of cloning (science), the plight of illegal aliens (social studies), themes of love and adversity (literature), and the question of whether artists should yield to public taste (the arts), are a few examples that compel students to think about freedom, human rights, and what it means to live in a democratic society.

Framing teaching and learning in a democratic context presents possibilities for many teachable moments. Whether the issue revolves around a dubious dance presentation or the use of discriminatory language, teachers can shift the focus from a localized problem to that which impacts the society at large. Such an approach moves away from moralizing and looks, instead, at the moral component from the standpoint of freedom and human rights.

Teaching for democratic practice, therefore, means that we look to the problematic as an opportunity for helping students broaden their vision beyond the immediate situation. It means that we value the potential of teachable moments within the recesses of a problematic situation. Most importantly, it means that we recognize the enormous growth potential from situations and issues that jeopardize students' rights to a safe, nurturing environment.

NOTES

1. Diane Ravitch, *The Death and Life of the Great American School System: How Testing and Choice are Undermining Education* (New York: Basic Books, 2010), 166.

2. Marguerite Vanden Wyngaard, "Culturally Responsive Pedagogies," in *Teaching City Kids: Understanding and Appreciating Them,* ed. Joe L. Kincheloe and kecia hayes (New York: Peter Lang, 2007), 121–129.

3. Deborah Meier, *In Schools We Trust: Creating Communities of Learning in an Era of Testing and Standardization* (Boston: Beacon, 2002).

4. Martin Haberman, *Star Teachers of Children in Poverty* (West Lafayette, IN: Kappa Delta Pi, 1995), 32.

5. Maxine Greene, *The Dialectic of Freedom* (New York: Teachers College Press, 1988), 134.

6. Joe L. Kincheloe, "City Kids—Not the Kind of Students You'd Want to Teach," in *Teaching City Kids: Understanding and Appreciating Them,* ed. Joe L. Kincheloe and kecia hayes (New York: Peter Lang, 2007), 5.

7. Mara Sapon-Shevin, "Teachable Moments for Social Justice," *Independent School* 67, no. 3 (2008).

Chapter Six

Teachable Moments, Part 2

A democracy is reciprocal and self-corrective, meaning that both its people and its social structures sustain each other while being always open to public scrutiny and evaluation. In a school, the reciprocal nature of democracy emerges from students and teachers working together in an environment of trust and respect. As self-corrective, a democratic classroom remains evolutionary; it allows for constant assessment of its effectiveness in providing joint decision making and equity among its participants.

A democracy is people-centered. It is a social context by which people work together to insure that human rights are upheld and that equal access to opportunities remains at the forefront of the governance structure. Teachers who engage in democratic practice must always be cognizant of the implications for social justice, which underlie decisions about curriculum and classroom behavior.

When classroom upheaval and disruption prevail, however, we can easily lose sight of the values that guide democratic practice. Even the most skilled and caring teachers can sometimes find themselves in a maelstrom of student discontent. In this situation, it is difficult to hang on to democratic values such as the freedom to voice one's opinion or the right to participate in joint decision making. This illuminates the delicate balance between the teacher and the student. When the teacher or the students dramatically override the other, the scale is tipped to favor the stronger, more powerful agent. This results either in autocratic teaching or classroom anarchy, both inimical to a healthy democracy.

A democracy cannot flourish in an environment in which students individually set rules of behavior. Neither can a democracy flourish when teachers refuse to allow students to ask appropriate thought-provoking questions or to involve students in meaningful decisions. "Schools must enforce standards of civility and teach students to respect themselves and others or they cannot provide a safe, orderly environment which is necessary for learning."[1]

At WGS, the lack of respect for teachers and schooling had reached a crisis level. Homeroom groupings (which stayed the same from class to class) had become toxic. Nothing—not a great lesson plan, not a discussion about the impact of the students' behavior on others, not a threat or reward, nor waiting for quiet—seemed to work for any teacher. Discipline problems had reached mammoth proportions and faculty morale fell exponentially.

November 30: *My students have returned to the coping mechanisms that I witnessed in the beginning of the year. Some students talk through the whole period. Others try to play cards. A few students attempt to read magazines under the desk and some just shriek periodically through the lesson. There is a steady flow of bathroom visits which gets longer and longer each time. Class discussions dwindle after thirty seconds. I am astounded at the level of awful behavior. In my opinion the school has regressed to a place where students call the shots.*

Marshall describes a similar scenario when he returned to teaching after several years as a supervisor, counselor, and administrator. He states, "What struck me immediately was the amount of inappropriate student behavior. Graffiti, rudeness, disrespect, and lack of interest in learning were prevalent. Although I was aware that society had changed, I had forgotten just how clearly students reflect the society in which they grow."[2]

There are a number of authors who believe that an important part of democratic practice involves teaching civility rather than just correcting behavior.[3] This means that teachers become agents in helping students develop internal check systems to monitor their own behavior. Whereas constantly correcting behavior puts the onus of responsibility in the hands of the teacher, it is far more valuable to develop classroom guidelines that place the onus of responsible behavior in the hands of the student. In theory, this kind of preparation for mature adulthood is irrefutable. How to do this in a classroom where students have developed disruptive habits is the larger question.

Marshall felt that social development plays a key role in developing democratic behaviors. With the assumption that responsible behavior is more cognitive than emotional, he developed a hierarchy of social behavior to help identify levels of social-emotional competencies. The hierarchy functions as a guide for both teachers and students in pinpointing behavior on a developmental scale. Because this may help teachers with similar problems, it is worth noting here:[4]

- (Levels 1 and 2) Anarchy and bossing/bullying. Society cannot exist without some norms, some external controls. A society becomes civil when its people cooperate and live according to these external influences.
- (Level 3) Conformity and/or cooperation.
- (Level 4) Democracy. As people grow, mature, cultivate manners, and develop values of right and wrong, the prompts for civility, originally external, become internalized. Doing the right thing simply because it is the right thing to do—without being asked or told . . . I refer to this level as democracy because taking the initiative to be responsible is an essential characteristic of self-rule.

This paradigm does not prescribe how to build a learning community but it does offer a concrete model for classifying behavior that contributes (or not) to a classroom democracy. If used as a barometer to help students develop an internal monitoring system, then one can feel confident about progressing toward a more democratic climate. If the model is used as a punitive tool or a way to humiliate students, the problems will escalate.

At WGS, rules and procedures seemed to change weekly. Most of the homeroom teachers had engaged students in formulating classroom rules, but following through was difficult since there was no common set of rules or procedures that governed the entire school. In short, there was a glaring lack of consistency in teaching students appropriate behavior for school.

Research demonstrates that while lack of consistency is hard for all students, it is especially harmful for urban adolescents whose lives are filled with significant stress. For instance, just getting to school can involve several busses, walks through unsafe neighborhoods, or navigation through the sheer numbers of people on cramped sidewalks or in tight living spaces. It is no wonder that urban students have highly sensitive trigger points to disruption and lack of routine in the school.

Along with these stressors, WGS itself was on a nosedive course. Instead of fixing the problems in the school itself, the head teacher, along with distraught support from other faculty members, decided to reconfigure the homerooms (students stayed in their homeroom grouping for every class). The strategy? Divide and conquer. At first it seemed like the perfect solution to the perfect storm. Take the most troublesome students and reassign them to other homerooms while reorganizing the classroom membership as well. In short, the students became chess pieces whose placement depended on compliance or rebelliousness. We thought we had created four harmonious, happy classrooms but no one foresaw the chaos and rage that would erupt when the students started school on Monday.

The students were furious. Having bonded as a group in their previous homerooms they were unhappy about changing their familial setting and angry that they had to deal with new power struggles and roles within the classroom. The new homeroom structures only redistributed the difficult students while setting up new problematic pairings with others. The academically successful students were the most distressed. They now had to cope with a new cohort that included a whole new set of dominant and aggressive personalities.

The rage spilled over into my class. Having no idea what I would encounter that Monday, I had planned a third lesson in a series of lessons on classical Indian music. Both the social studies teacher and language arts teacher were teaching about the culture and geography of India. We hoped that an interdisciplinary unit would help students learn about India through various perspectives.

> December 1: *The first class was pretty limp and sullen. The second class, however, took me to task. Melissa angrily told me that she was SICK of all this Indian stuff and why were all the teachers doing the same thing? I countered with the fact that we weren't doing the same thing at all but we were each presenting different ways of looking at India. Melissa shot back with "We can't keep anything straight . . . you are overloading us with information." At this point I lost my cool and the students were now suiting up in riot gear. The students screamed at each other back and forth and hurled accusations at me regarding my teaching practice, how I decided what to teach, and why they couldn't just learn what they liked. The students were out of control and I knew that I wasn't going to pull them back any time soon. My mind was in a state of panic . . . "What do I do?" "How can I get control?" "They hate me."*

Fortunately we had reached the end of this tortuous class and I had a lunch break to work out my mixed feelings. On one hand I was terribly hurt and upset but on the other hand I knew I couldn't blame the students. They actually made some excellent points along the way, albeit not very nicely. Although I wanted to blame the students, I also realized that I must have developed some measure of trust in that students felt free to vent their frustration. How could I chastise them for speaking their minds? As one student pointed out, "This is a democracy."

Was this a democracy? Does a democratic classroom give students the right to shout and scream whatever they want? Here is a classic example of why many teachers resist teaching strategies and classroom venues that border on what they perceive as "democratic" or, in more simplistic terms, unfettered freedom. Yet our American democratic structure, with all of its human rights, does establish boundaries on behavior. Precisely where we draw the line is sometimes legislated or sometimes an issue for future legislation. Our founding fathers envisioned a critically thinking populace where problems were carefully examined and anarchy lessened by an intricate set of checks and balances.

In terms of schooling, Michelli states, "One of the broader ways to think about education for democracy is to consider the 'civil' responsibilities of individuals."[5] What does it mean to be civil as a participant in a democratic society? How does one deal with disagreements and resolve them? Learning to be respectful does not mean accepting all positions put forth as equally valid. Further, "We want students to be engaged civically [sic] and act civilly, but we want them to do so in the context of good, well-formed judgments."[6]

Michelli gives insight into an important, but often overlooked point, about building the democratic structures of a classroom: civil behavior is fundamental to civic behavior. We cannot grow a democracy when students are disrespectful to one another or to the teacher. Without a sense of civility, students can neither hold a productive conversation nor behave in ways that support the growth of others in the class. The teacher, as part of this community, has the same rights to respectful behavior as the rest of the students. Without respect for "the other," the wheel continues to turn in place.

While this may seem like common sense to any teacher, the goals for creating a civil classroom vary. Some teachers want a peaceful classroom so that they can teach without constant interruption. Teachers engaged in democratic practice, however, have additional goals. They know that the classroom is a microcosm for society and that creating a classroom where students respect each other becomes an important part of the educative process that leads to responsible adulthood.[7]

A large part of students respecting other students is the ability to see through someone else's eyes—to feel oneness with the human condition. We may complain about a student's lack of sensitivity but we rarely talk about how to teach for empathy. If teachers truly care for their students they understand that empathic behavior on the part of the student is not automatic, but must be cradled and massaged throughout the teaching process. In fact, many educators believe that the teaching of self-control, social participation, and interest in others not only warrants a special place in the curriculum but are the "bedrock of schooling" itself.[8]

Far beyond the conceptual details that form the core of a discipline, teaching students to recognize hurtful actions from the victim's perspective and reconcile accordingly goes a long way toward developing habits of mind and heart. The increasing ability to manage emotions and social relationships is not only essential for a peaceable community of learners but is key for success in the workplace and effective leadership as well.[9]

With this in mind, I thought about how I would handle the next lesson with this particular class. Clearly the events that took place had to be addressed, but how? On one hand, they needed to know that expressing their opinions was a good thing. On the other hand, freedom of speech comes with responsibilities. Screaming to out-shout other students and with no sense of order was completely reprehensible.

I must have gone over my opening lines a thousand times but when I actually stood in front of the class, I found myself speaking straight from the heart.

> December 5: *I began to talk about how much I believed in the democratic system. And, for that reason, I very much valued their individual points of view. Freedom, however, comes at a price. "Your words have an impact on people and indiscriminate insults are hurtful and painful. That's just how I felt yesterday. I felt deeply hurt."*

There wasn't much discussion but I knew they were listening very carefully. When I finished several students offered a public apology for the class. At the end of class, Desiree walked in from another classroom and demanded, "Is this the class that made Dr. D. so upset?" She followed with a barrage of threats as only Desiree can do so well.

The entire incident, from the beginning to end, became the catalyst for teaching students to see and respond to the range of human feelings. After the previous class they knew that something was wrong but they didn't understand why I might be upset. So many of them experience only yelling and hitting as a way of communication. In essence, what started out as every teacher's horror ended as a heart-rending teachable moment.

Teaching students to empathize is part of our responsibility as good teachers. While empathy and democracy may seem like a strange pairing in the language of schooling, a healthy democracy does depend on the ability to appreciate another's perspective. It is impossible to make thoughtful decisions for the benefit of the group if one is only focused on his/her own needs.

Modeling empathy, on the teacher's part, is a first step in helping students identify empathic behavior. It is important, though, that teachers go further and consciously teach students to put themselves in another's shoes, not in a punitive manner but as part of teaching students to function in society. According to Dewey, "Such a society must have a type of education which gives individuals a personal interest in social relationships and control, and the habits of mind which secure social changes without introducing disorder."[10]

Goodlad identifies four key dimensions of teaching as democratic practice: (1) enculturating children into a democratic society, (2) providing access to knowledge for all, (3) striving to advance social justice in the schools (stewardship), and (4) enhancing learning through nurturing pedagogy.[11] The last dimension, nurturing pedagogy, plays a central role in helping students become compassionate, caring human beings. Nurturing pedagogy hinges on a theory of caring for students and about students. This reciprocal nature of caring is essential to a democratic classroom.

The role of caring has been discussed in previous chapters from the standpoint of how teachers relate to their students. This chapter, however, examines caring in terms of how teachers can help students care for each other. Writings on caring in education tend to take two different paths. The first is caring as a giving process—a one-way relationship from teacher to student. [12] That is, the teacher cares for the student's welfare by building relationships based on trust and meeting his/her needs socially and academically. Nel Noddings, however, believes that caring is and must be a reciprocal process. In this second approach, students learn how to give care as well as receive care. [13]

Although many authors focus on the teacher as the primary caregiver, and indeed this was the thrust of chapter 4, Noddings asserts that students must also learn to give care in order to grow empathically: "My contention is, first that we should want more from our educational efforts than adequate academic achievement and, second, that we will not achieve even that meager success unless our children believe that they themselves are cared for and learn to care for others." [14] She asserts that the study and practice of caring need to take place at all levels of schooling, including the secondary school.

Teacher modeling is primary to building an ethic of care in the classroom. Often, novice teachers don't recognize caring as something different from love. In order to help students learn to care for each other, teachers can not only devise lessons that focus on receiving and giving care but must also recognize teachable moments as they arise in the classroom.

For instance, with a student who has difficulties managing his anger, one might ask in a private conversation, "With your own friends, how do you show that you care about them?" "What are some ways that you could manage your anger as a means of caring for others in the class, even those that you don't like very much?" The key, here, is helping the student recognize his/her caring instincts with friends as a basis for extending that care to other people.

Other ways of teaching caring require the teacher to bring out the human element in course content. In this sense, one teaches the language of care through academic content. For example, to read *The Diary of Anne Frank* from a deep level of understanding, one must be able to empathize with loss—loss of fundamental human rights, loss of significant relationships, and loss of identity.

Finding appropriate ways to focus on different kinds of loss helps students better identify with the courage that Anne Frank exhibits throughout her diary. Here, the teacher designs questions and projects that help students focus on the empathic elements of Anne's story as a framework for understanding the human condition. Although one could teach the book only through its historical context, teaching both the history and the human dimension might provide a more profound experience while also helping students uncover the empathic core within themselves.

When educating pre-service students, teachers will find it worth the effort to approach democratic practice from a framework of care and empathy. Stories from the teacher educator's experience or vignettes from student field experiences help to authenticate pedagogical theory. As a teaching device, stories are a great way to humanize theory as students tend to remember and draw on these examples as reference points when faced with challenging situations in the classroom. Reflective journals also help students identify and process the role of caring in the learning situation. As mentioned in previous chapters, communities of learning are also tangible experiences for giving and receiving care.

Developing positive social relationships and respect for the self and others needs a central position in the curriculum.[15] The daily social relationships of students provide many opportunities for addressing care for others. In addition, teachers in a democratic classroom understand that caring for humanity, whether discussing the plight of Native Americans in the 1800s or an insulting remark to another child, cannot take place in a meaningful way if students do not respect themselves or others.

Can a test-driven public afford teachers the space they need to teach the heart as well as the mind? In order for this to take place, stakeholders must recognize that the teaching of caring not only lends itself to a safe environment but advances learning in other areas as well. "Caring and compassion are not soft mushy goals. They are part of the hard core of subjects we are responsible for teaching. . . . The capacity to see the world as others might is central to unsentimental compassion and at the root of both intellectual skepticism and empathy."[16] Thus, teachers need to not only teach content but also to teach social and emotional human development.

What does a classroom look like when students and teachers engage in reciprocal caring? First, teachers and students develop relationships based on trust and respect as a foundation for the give and take nature of caring. Second, the classroom must be guided by a set of rules to which all agree as important for the sanctity of social interaction. Third, when problems arise, the teacher recognizes the need to process conflicts with the class or individual students. And fourth, the teacher is careful in designing a curriculum that provides for student diversity and allows access of knowledge to all.

Teacher educators can do more to underscore the importance of care and empathy in the learning process. Most focus primarily on teaching content or delivering information about schooling, for example, educational philosophy.

In terms of classroom management, teacher educators spend inadequate time discussing how to set boundaries that establish control in the urban classroom.

It seems to me, though, that the terms "behavior management" and "control" do not belong on the same page with "teaching for caring." While we want to develop students' internal locus of control to avoid constant reliance on correction or a reward system for shaping behavior, we also want students who not only cooperate with others but also go out into the world with a sense of compassion, dignity, and humanity. The goal, in democratic practice, is not to autocratically control students but to teach ways of living in a community both in and out of school.

"Learning to develop an environment conducive for mutual respect and 'we-ness' with students should begin in the first teacher preparation class."[17] The concept of "we-ness" is simple in theory but highly complex in practice. Fundamentally, all students need order and safety in the school. Ideally the faculty and administration work together as a whole to maintain guidelines for building respectful relationships in a schooling environment. But faculties and administration do not always support the same goals. Our setting at WGS reflected this problem.

When I think about our challenging students at WGS, I believe that we knew little about the needs of urban children and often felt immobilized by their behavior. Contributing to this feeling of immobilization was a dichotomy in the way our head teacher felt she was demonstrating care by loudly demanding that students show more respect, and many of us who wanted to show care in a different way. The type of caring, such as telling students when they have done a good job, acknowledging helpful feedback during a lesson, or getting to know the student on a one-on-one basis, reflected a one-way caring paradigm. With the exception of a few students, we were burning out trying to care without receiving any care in return.

If the predilection in teaching is to view caring as a one-way relationship, then teachers carry the sole burden of caring. Caring as a reciprocal relationship, however, comes closer to the ideal of democratic practice in the school. With reciprocal caring students develop empathy for each other, understand that people have different perspectives, and respect those differences among us. When we teach students to care, we also teach them to celebrate the "we-ness" of society. This then lends itself to the development of sensibilities for social justice as students begin to recognize inequities that weaken a democracy. According to Noddings:

Caring is not just a warm, fuzzy feeling that makes people kind and likable. Caring implies a continuous search for competence. . . . To have as our educational goal the production of caring, competent, loving and lovable people is not anti-intellectual. Rather it demonstrates respect for the full range of human talents.[18]

Creating an environment of reciprocal caring, like any trust-building experience, takes time and commitment. It involves developing a social curriculum in tandem with the academic curriculum. Designing a social curriculum then leads to deliberate teaching of civil behavior and empathy for others in and outside the classroom. The process is not clean and neat. In her chapter, "Building Community from Chaos," Christensen argues that a "classroom community isn't always synonymous with warmth and harmony . . . a real community is forged out of struggle."[19] This is the stuff that beginning teachers need to know—that the struggle, the arguments, and the tears are part of the process to connect with one another.

Beginning teachers also need to know that caring for one another is not an automatic disposition nor does caring necessarily look the same in all households. Urban students often come from a family in which a strong authoritative parent/caregiver is viewed as a type of caring. Other students come from situations where care is not modeled. To establish a reciprocal caring model, teachers must not only understand how students experience care in other settings, but also learn from direct teaching that uses the language of care, such as, "We listen to others because we care about what they have to say," "We respect our classroom rules and routines because it provides a safe space for us to learn."

In essence, the curriculum, methods of teaching, and ways of assessing students are an effort to answer the question, "What does it mean to educate?" In a classroom framed by democratic practice, academic content and reciprocal caring are intertwined. Teachers demonstrate care in the content that they choose and in the relationships that they build with their students. Students show care in the way they acknowledge different points of view and the sensitivity they show their classmates and teachers.

Linda Darling-Hammond writes, "Growing up as humane and decent people who can appreciate others and take satisfaction in doing things well requires schools that allow for humanity and decency, that cultivate appreciation, that support deep learning about things that matter to the people in them."[20] It is the "people in them" that we acutely need to know and to teach our students to know. A democratic classroom that emanates caring and mindfulness is a precious gift that opens the door to all things possible. This is why we care for our students and why our students must care for each other.

NOTES

1. Diane Ravitch, *The Death and Life of the Great American School System: How Testing and Choice are Undermining Education* (New York: Basic Books, 2010), 241.

2. Marvin Marshall and Kerry Weisner, "Using a Discipline System to Promote Learning," *Phi Delta Kappan* 85, no. 7 (2004): 498.

3. See Linda Christensen, "Building Community from Chaos," in *City Kids, City Schools: More Reports from the Front Row,* ed. William Ayers, Gloria Ladson-Billings, Gregory Michie, and Pedro A. Noguera (New York: The New Press, 2008), 60–73.

4. Marshall and Weisner, "Using a Discipline System," 499–500.

5. Nicholas M. Michelli, "Education for Democracy: What Can It Be?" in *Teacher Education for Democracy and Social Justice,* ed. Nicholas M. Michelli and David Lee Keiser (New York: Routledge, 2005), 5.

6. Michelli, "Education for Democracy," 5.

7. Maurice J. Elias, Joseph E. Zins, Roger P. Weissberg, Karin S. Frey, Mark T. Greenberg, Norris M. Haynes, Rachel Kessler, Mary E. Schwab-Stone, and Timothy R. Shriver, *Promoting Social and Emotional Learning: Guidelines for Educators* (Alexandria, VA: Association for Supervision and Curriculum Development, 1997).

8. Nel Noddings, "Teaching Themes of Care," *Phi Delta Kappan* 76, no. 9 (1995): 675–679.

9. Elias, et al., *Promoting Social and Emotional Learning,* 2–7.

10. John Dewey, *Democracy and Education* (Middlesex, England: Echo Library, 2007), 76.

11. John I. Goodlad, *Educational Renewal: Better Teachers, Better Schools* (San Francisco: Jossey-Bass, 1994), 4–5.

12. See, for example, Ruben Garza, "Latino and White High School Students' Perception of Caring Behaviors: Are We Culturally Responsive to Our Students?" *Urban Education* 44 (2009): 297–321. doi: 10.1177/0042085908318714; Jessica T. Shiller, "These Are Our Children!: An Examination of Relationship-Building Practices in Urban High Schools," *Urban Review* 41 (2009): 461–485. doi: 001:10.1007/s11256-008-0110-1.

13. Nel Noddings, *The Challenge to Care in Schools,* 2nd ed. (New York: Teachers College Press, 2005).

14. Noddings, "Teaching Themes of Care," 675.

15. Ruth Sidney Charney, *Teaching Children to Care: Management in the Responsive Classroom* (Greenfield, MA: Northeast Foundation for Children, 1992).

16. Deborah Meier, *In Schools We Trust: Creating Communities of Learning in an Era of Testing and Standardization* (Boston: Beacon Press, 2002), 63.

17. Melba Venison, "Effective Teacher Training Programs for Urban School Teachers," in *Best Practices for Teaching Students in Urban Schools,* ed. Rose M. Duhon-Sells, Magellan Studies in Education, vol. 100 (Lewistown, NY: The Edwin Mellen Press, 2004), 49.

18. Noddings, "Teaching Themes of Care," 676.

19. Linda Christensen, "Building Community from Chaos," in *City Kids, City Schools: More Reports from the Front Row,* ed. William Ayers, Gloria Ladson-Billings, Gregory Michie, and Pedro A. Noguera (New York: The New Press, 2008), 61.

20. Linda Darling-Hammond, "Education, Equity, and the Right to Learn," in *The Public Purpose of Education and Schooling,* ed. John I. Goodlad and Timothy J. McMannon (San Francisco: Jossey-Bass, 1997), 44.

Chapter Seven

Mid-Year Reflection

We are fortunate, as teachers, to have several lengthy holidays (winter break, summer, etc.) that other professions are not generally permitted. Although some outside of the teaching profession complain about "summers off," they may not realize that many teachers continue to work at their craft during these breaks. Good teachers see professional development as pockets of time for engaging in pedagogical reading, workshops, and graduate courses rather than as extra, unwanted work. These breaks provide well-deserved respites for distancing oneself from the classroom in order to reflect on particular students or develop new skills. With this in mind, chapter 7 takes a slight turn from the previous chapters in order to examine interesting writings about what makes adolescents tick.

The phrase "know your students" has been a recurring mantra in the literature. As one continues to read, there is a growing realization that the concept of knowing means so much more than familiarity. Knowing an urban teenager demands that the teacher understand something about adolescent development, what it means to grow up in the inner city, how race impacts social development, and the challenges of poverty. Although each of these issues is a book in itself, this chapter serves as a starting point for future reading.

LABELS, STEREOTYPES, AND OTHER CHALLENGES

Garza writes that teachers repeatedly misinterpret students' uniqueness and strengths as problems and complex challenges. "As a result, educators often label students as unmotivated, withdrawn, or academically incapable."[1] This one-dimensional view of students has ramifications for the narrowness in which many teachers approach instruction and the impatience with which they respond to youth. Unfortunately, what students do outside the classroom, their interests and passions, their cultural identity, and their home life is not always considered an important part of the academic process. According to Ayers and Alexander-Tanner, we cannot adequately serve our students without viewing each student as *three-dimensional*.[2] That is, students have a classroom persona which is inextricably intertwined with the events that happen at home and outside the home.

There are countless external risk factors that impact on a student's work in school. Whereas children from more affluent circumstances come to school with an experientially rich background enhanced, for instance, by travel, arts classes, and trips to the library, poor children's experiences are often limited to rides on the bus or subway, colorful pictures on cereal boxes, and long stretches in front of the television. Their cramped, run-down homes rarely provide the privacy of a personal bedroom where they can read or do homework.[3] In fact, school may be the only place where students have the opportunity to eat nourishing food. The things that many of us take for granted, such as clean air, peace and quiet, and open spaces, are not an ordinary part of life in the "ghetto."[4]

Steinberg has written extensively about urban teaching. Her statements below reflect a snapshot of adolescents growing up in the city. Being a poor urban student means:

- Transportation is difficult and you have to use a public bus or subway and be there to catch it at just the right time—otherwise, you miss school.
- Children live in a rented house and have free or reduced-price lunches.
- Parents have long days at work.
- Adolescents have limited opportunity to belong to sports teams.
- Families suffer through traffic congestion and wake to the sounds of garbage trucks and car alarms.
- Adolescents and adults are often depicted as a criminals, gangsters, or losers in the media.
- Families are bad because they are from the inner city.[5]

It is not fair to suggest that poor youth uniformly endure all of the circumstances listed above but, as a general composite, many of these statements ring true for poor urban adolescents. Life in the city creates unique physical and psychological burdens that students bring into the classroom. Some signs of stress include antagonism toward school, rebelliousness, lack of respect for themselves and educators, high rates of absenteeism, and lack of academic or vocational goals.[6] Further, these characterizations are compounded by public generalizations that urban adolescents as lazy and indifferent to school.

This kind of stereotyping creeps through the media, winds its way into family conversations, and filters through social institutions. Those living in poverty are constantly labeled with "grossly, deficit-laden characteristics that put them at risk of being viewed as less capable, less cultural, and less worthy as learners."[7] As with all stereotypes, the negative social perception of minority youth (especially Black and Latino youth) is not only blatantly exaggerated but also gives tacit permission to accept inequitable education as the norm.[8]

Most discouraging are the many teachers who believe that African American or Latino students are incapable of high-level work. Statistics show that students of color are overrepresented in both special needs classes and disciplinary referrals.[9] Moreover, teachers often view leaders among students of color as disruptive, aggressive, and low achievers.[10]

Much of the research, particularly on Black students, takes the perspective that students of color are deficient in many areas associated with success in school.[11] This translates to students as unprepared or unable to cope with academic rigor and, therefore, in constant need of remediation. Consequently, teachers are less likely to teach with the imagination and rigor that these students deserve.

One of the problematic fallouts of a deficit point of view is that it places the blame for inadequate performance directly on the students and their families rather than the inadequacies of the school and society at large.[12] The poor conditions and apartheid-like nature of urban schools has been well documented.[13] Although some cities have created new, modern spaces for learning, the majority of American urban schools are neglected and resource-impoverished. Urban children simply do not have access to the same educational opportunities as children from more affluent homes.

In contrast to a deficit perspective, some contemporary researchers have begun to define adolescent development from the standpoint of key strengths and resiliency rather than problems to fix. According to this research, the five Cs—competence, confidence, connection, character, and caring—reflect more realistic benchmarks for assessing student growth.[14] From a teacher's perspective, this approach focuses on the positive qualities of each child, placing emphasis on the individual rather than a generalized grouping practice.

In general, schools are especially good at sorting and labeling children. Although academic policies may try to avoid tracking students by ability, the fact is that poor, minority children are often unwittingly tracked either by an overindulgence in special needs/remedial programs or by the uninformed decisions that teachers make. The challenge for teachers, then, is to reappraise the theory that Black and Latino students come to school with well-entrenched deficits and build, instead, upon the strengths that they bring to the classroom. This, however, is particularly difficult in a system that embraces standardization as its primary yardstick for assessing students.

IDENTITY FORMATION IN ADOLESCENCE

Adolescence is a fragile time for all students but particularly for students of color. During this stage of life, adolescents not only begin to develop their own identity but also recognize that "membership within a racial category requires certain social and political commitments."[15] Teachers in racially integrated schools may notice that friendships begin to form more closely along racial lines.[16] As students enter adolescence, crossing racial boundaries can become problematic. With increasing awareness of the group differences, students of color generally become concerned with how their peers will react to their participation in interracial relationships.[17]

Identity for students of color is a journey toward selfhood that goes beyond the complexities of "Who am I?," to "Who am I as a Black or Latino person?"[18] "Where do I fit in a Eurocentric society?" and "How is my identity connected to my success in school?" According to Goldstein, "Adolescent identity construction is a function of many experiences, both personal cultural, in which young people create meanings about themselves and the world in which they live."[19] The complexity of adolescent development has been the subject of much research and lies well beyond the scope of this book. It is clear, though, that identity formation involves an interaction of many components.

Swanson, for instance, identifies three interlaced factors: the context in which students live and go to school, the way that adolescents perceive and respond to this context, and the level of maturational development.[20] This means that identity for many urban adolescents involves a context of poverty and how adolescents respond to the challenges of living in poverty.

Race also plays a large role in identity formation, as students of color must constantly shift between their culture and that of the dominant White society.[21] According to a Chicago teen, as referenced in *From Our America* by LeAlan Jones with David Isay: "We live in two different Americas. In the ghetto, our laws are totally different, our language is totally different, and our lives are totally different."[22]

A large part of one's identity formation takes place in school. In the face of societal criticism, urban adolescents struggle to develop a positive identity as competent learners. Unfortunately statistics seem to portray these students as failures. For instance, only half of the Black and Latino student population graduates from high school.[23] The dropout rate for Black and Latino students far exceeds that of White students. This leads to the misguided assumption that Black and Latino youth lack the intelligence and motivation to succeed in school. As Duncan-Andrade and Morrell write, "In most urban schools, students are taught to under-value, or worse, to devalue their own experiences. Without a strong sense of self-respect in the context of school and society, it is virtually impossible for a person to engage in the praxis of self-realization."[24]

Why is it, then, that some students of color have the resiliency to stay in school despite difficult odds when others cannot find a meaningful connection? Flores-González spent a year in an urban high school studying the characteristics of students who stay in school and earn a diploma versus those who leave.[25] The "stayers" were students who had involvement in school activities, were connected to one or more adults, and could articulate plans for the future. Because peer approval is so important to identity formation, it stands to reason that clubs or collaborative projects have the potential for providing positive ties to school. Connections with adults are also important because adults can help students construct realistic future goals.

The "leavers," on the other hand, were students who derived prestige and feelings of self-worth from peers outside of the school. In school, they often exhibited an "attack mode" posture, looking for reasons to fight or explode over any perceived slight. Leavers do not believe that a diploma would bring anything more than a low-paying job. Consequently, they reflect the greatest susceptibility for dropping out of school.

Given Flores-González's findings, educators might facilitate the development of a positive school identity by understanding the importance of students' finding their own niche. Urban settings often offer fewer opportunities for after-school activities and clubs than suburban schools. Yet adolescents need to find places in school where they are appreciated and valued. Opportunities to work as a team, whether putting together a fund-raising event or participating in sports activities, help develop connections with friends and teachers. The main objective is to help students form a trusting attachment to school.

Competence in school also comes from doing well on traditionally accepted achievement measures such as class participation, projects, and tests. "Understanding the process through which racial identities are constructed in school is essential if we are to devise strategies that can transform the ways in which race and achievement become linked."[26] Throughout the nation, however, many Black students have consistently performed lower than White students. This achievement gap has been the subject of much debate, citing arguments that range from schools not addressing the cultural difference of students of color to the perception that school only embraces White values.

Much has been written about "acting White" as it relates to a Eurocentric value of achievement in schooling. "Acting White" behaviors include "speaking standard English, having white friends, listening to 'white people's music,' walking a particular way, and refusing to adopt particularly 'black' ways of doing things."[27] Many believe that Black students consciously reject "the good student" image because it signifies submission to White standards and values.

Probably the most often cited research on the relationship between "acting White" and academic achievement is by Nigerian American anthropologist John Ogbu. His research suggests that Black students must accept White values to achieve in school.[28] Although many in education continue to promulgate the ideas of his research, some authors have widely questioned whether one can reduce the complexity of academic identity to a single factor (race).

Interestingly, one study found that African American students who scored high on measures of Afrocentric identity also scored high on achievement measures.[29] Conversely, those who scored high on measures of Eurocentric identity showed low achievement in school. For African American students, this would suggest that a strong sense of racial identity actually *contributes* to strong school performance. This particular study, then, challenges the idea that students must adopt White values in order to achieve in school.

In a study with urban Latino students, findings showed that feelings of confidence and competence were linked to the student's identity with a vocation.[30] That is, students who had clear ideas about what they wanted to do after high school scored highest on tests of confidence and competence. They were better able to define their goals, strengths, and interests regarding vocational aspirations. If accurate, teacher guidance in persuading students to plan for the future may have a strong impact on their motivation to succeed in school.

One of the most powerful ways for teachers to help students mature is to teach them how to cope with negative messages about their ability and their culture. Lashing out or holding in anger are coping mechanisms that, while understandable, are unhealthy for the student as well as the classroom. Students who remain silent, on the other hand, may be exhibiting compliance. This not only erodes self-confidence but plants seed of discontent that may result in future explosive responses to the slightest provocation. Although passive behavior is more easily overlooked than loud, confrontational behavior, both need teacher attention.

The term "resistance" is often used to describe ways that students of color respond to racially biased stress. Students can counteract overt or covert threats to their cultural identity by moving in at least one of two directions. These threats can either provide the fuel for bursts of aggression or assist in the development of a critical consciousness regarding the role of race in

American society. Although parents play a large part, positively or negatively, in enculturating their children to the challenges of negotiating the currently White-dominant society, teachers also have the power to help students develop positive resistance tactics.

The first step in helping students is to acknowledge the presence of social injustices and their impact on students of color. Many teachers, however, shy away from discussions of race, oppression, or other socially relevant issues for fear of treading outside politically safe boundaries. It takes courage to initiate class discussions that address forms of bias or illuminate such injustice through content (e.g., themes of racism in *To Kill A Mockingbird* or the challenges that Marion Anderson faced as a Black singer of art music) or discuss a race-related school incident. However, the recognition that racism exists in American society is a critical move forward.

Teachers can do a great service to their students by helping them identify positive action for opposing racially biased behavior. Mirón states, "City kids adopt passive resistance because they do not have the knowledge of skills to exercise political change."[31] Students, in other words, need both appropriate language and the understanding of how the system works to effect political change. Whether challenging a school district's policy to stay in session on Martin Luther King Day or petitioning for more assemblies to celebrate Black and Latino cultures, political action may seem daunting to teachers.

However, in smaller but no less important ways, teachers can help frame language for addressing hurtful or cruel remarks in daily encounters. Rather than avoiding issues of social justice, teachers should understand that "recognizing and making sense of social injustice and oppression is a fundamental part of social individuality."[32] Helping students develop resilience may be a teacher's greatest gift to students of color. Students with high self-esteem and a feeling of competence are more likely to persevere in the face of extreme challenges such as poverty than those who feel victimized and vulnerable.[33] Positive resistance tactics, such as peaceful protests or letters to the school newspaper, often build confidence while affirming cultural identity. Noguera writes, "Understanding the process through which racial identities are constructed in school is essential if we are to devise strategies that can transform the ways in which race and achievement become linked."[34]

Fundamentally, schools should be safe places where students' strengths are encouraged and their differences celebrated, especially for those prone to failure. The role of the teacher/school in facilitating feelings of high self-worth cannot be emphasized enough. These are among the many factors in which teachers can make a difference in the adolescent's search for identity.

URBAN ADOLESCENT MALES

"African American males are perhaps the most highly stigmatized and stereotyped group in American society."[35] Criticized for speech patterns, dress, or lack of eye contact, African American males bear the brunt of school discipline referrals and placements in remedial classrooms.[36] Accordingly, research demonstrates that schools also tend to label and sort Black males more frequently than other students. This practice denies full access to the kind of education provided to other students and reflects tracking of the worst kind. Ironically, most Black males do value school and want to succeed.[37]

The "great fear" for many teachers has to do with classroom control—that African American males are confrontational and hard to control.[38] In addition, there is a prevailing mindset that Black males are failures as students, as fathers, and as husbands. This affects not only how teachers perceive and respond to these students, but the student's development of self-esteem as well.

When Black or Latino males believe that they are misunderstood and failed by the educational system, they often develop unhealthy coping mechanisms that actually confirm outside prejudice and bias. For instance, Black males often sabotage themselves by acting out in the classroom or avoiding high achievement in their studies.[39] Sometimes they perceive these behaviors as the only way to guard manhood, especially when it appears that the school doesn't understand their behavior or achievements.[40]

The perception of Black and Latino males as hostile or defiant reinforces the notion that urban adolescents are not to be trusted. Author of *The Trouble with Black Boys,* Noguero states that "it is easy for adults to misinterpret and misunderstand the attitudes and behavior of young people. Generational difference, especially when compounded by difference in race and class, often make it difficult for adults to communicate effectively with youth."[41]

One of the most insidious risks that urban males face is the temptation or threat to join gangs. Students are drawn to gangs believing that they lack respect in schools or are powerless to make changes in their home or school situations.[42] Gang membership offers protection, respect, and a pseudo-family environment. These are areas that males often see as serious voids in their lives. Many urban youths feel that gang membership is inevitable. To males of color, gang membership often signifies a necessary rite of passage into adulthood.[43] For this reason, choosing a gang orientation over that which characterizes the "good student" can seem inevitable.[44]

It is crucial for teachers to recognize the two most salient features of gang membership: loyalty and respect. Because the literature suggests that males often perceive schools as not taking them seriously, teachers must understand that students of color, especially males, hold respect as paramount to their identity. Therefore, any actions that run counter to the respect that males feel they deserve can create a situation where urban males believe that they must defend themselves. This can create not only power struggles between the student and teacher, but also acting-out behavior in the classroom or hallways.

Teacher education rarely deals with the impact of gangs in schooling. Although much of gang behavior is underground and outside the school, there is enough information available on Black, Latino, and Asian gangs to educate pre-service teachers more thoroughly. In an attempt to reduce gang influence, for instance, most schools ban the wearing of gang colors and particular head wear. However, it is more important that pre-service teachers understand how students can be seriously threatened to join gangs or, conversely, highly attracted to the "benefits" that gangs have to offer.

The need for respect, and the feeling that this is not honored in the classroom, contributes to Black/Latino students' growing mistrust of schools. This presents a formidable challenge for teachers. While they may not have the power to counteract street activity, teachers do have a prodigious opportunity to help teens examine the choices that they make, especially when teens feel that they have no choice. The more teachers reach out to urban youth and respect them for who they are, the more likely students may see school as a positive space rather than a dumping ground for unruly or unintelligent students.

Acknowledging that many students of color encounter unfathomable risks in their lives, however, is not an excuse for aggressive, disrespectful behavior in the school. Just as in academic situations, teachers must also set high standards school behavior. A teacher simply cannot help the student succeed if constantly involved in a battle of wills. When cognizant of the challenges that urban adolescents face, especially Black and Latino males, teachers may approach discipline differently.

Teachers who understand the importance of male identity formation are in a better position to understand that seemingly dysfunctional behavior is not always grounds for harsh punishment or placement in lower-level classes. Nor is it reasonable to generalize that all urban males exhibit a negative response to school. There are many urban teens for whom street life is not the basis for their identity. While the urban environment cannot help but influence identity development, it does not necessarily impact on teens in similar ways. Many urban students do enjoy school and recognize that education is a path toward avoiding the pitfalls of street life.

In short, urban male students particularly depend upon teachers to meet them where they are. They need understanding teachers in their lives who refuse to believe that inappropriate behavior equals disdain for adults or schooling. They also need teachers who make informed decisions about how and when students need attention in their classroom work rather than place-ment in remedial classes. From this perspective, teachers can have an immense role in shaping the male's view of himself as a competent learner and an agent of change in life decisions.

URBAN ADOLESCENT GIRLS

As with urban males, urban females are also subjected to a range of negative stereotypes. Some of the common terms associated with urban females include: welfare mother, pregnant teenager, victim of domestic abuse, drug addict, and unmotivated student.[45] Tolman states that "the parochial association of sexuality with the Urban Girl is a disservice to all other girls, whose sexuality is not identified as important or even existent."[46] On the other hand, urban girls must not only confront the challenges of sexism but also racism, classism, and the dominance of a White society.

Research on female adolescent development is just beginning to emerge as an important field of study. Although most of the research addresses Caucasian girls, a limited number of recent studies have begun to focus on a more ethnically diverse population. Nevertheless, there are things to be learned from the entire body of research.

In terms of White girls, some research on adolescent development suggests a "Queen Bee" syndrome where girls vie for an attachment to the most popular girl.[47] Because females are socially encouraged to avoid outward signs of aggression, many carry out their negative responses to other girls "underground." Backbiting, exclusion, rumors, name calling, and manipulation to cause psychological pain reflect some of the ways in which girls humiliate or "get even" with other girls.[48]

Tatum writes, "Though Black girls living in the context of a larger Black community may have more social choices, they too have to contend with devaluing messages about who they are and who they will become, especially if they are poor or working-class."[49] In the Black culture, parents tend to socialize girls toward assertiveness and aggression in order to combat institutionalized racism. While teachers often categorize Black females as "loud and disruptive," in many cases girls feel that "they can only make themselves heard by using physical force or dangerous speech."[50] Paradoxically, these are the very behaviors that schools and teachers try to curb.

Part of helping students develop healthy relationships is making them aware of the relational consequences of aggressive and manipulative behavior. The teacher's role is socializing students to recognize that they can control alternative aggressions.[51] Rather than viewing aggressive behavior as a deficit, some authors believe that these challenges offer an opportunity to develop an adolescent's "critical conscience." That is, by resisting structural oppression or racial slurs in appropriate ways, urban females begin to develop an assertiveness that nurtures resilience rather than victimization. [52]

The crux of Latino culture, on the other hand, is the centrality of the family. The concept of family extends not only to immediate relations but extended family as well. In the Latino family, the male is considered the dominant member. The family structure emphasizes female submission, respect, and obedience. [53] While males are expected to protect the female both physically and economically, females are socialized to take on the role as wife and mother. [54]

In addition to domestic responsibilities, the mother takes a strong position in warning her daughter(s) to avoid early sexual activity. Paradoxically, this means that "girls are asked to both care for and respect men while at the same time holding them suspect because of their predatory sexuality." [55] In trying to juggle these conflicting messages, Latina girls may experience depression and sadness. Teachers should note that depression is often *more* acceptable than confrontations between the adolescent girl and her family. [56]

Given the fact that Latino girls, as with White girls, often suppress their feelings of anger, one might conclude that these females would benefit from learning to assert themselves. However, when American education encourages individualism, it sends conflicting messages to Latina girls who are socialized for a different role in the family. Taylor points out, "Encouraging healthy resistance in the form of 'speaking out' may lead to hurtful conflicts between mothers and daughters." [57] Nevertheless, teachers need to help Latino females find their voice in a context that does not create additional stress between the family and the adolescent.

In terms of schooling, the literature indicates that Latinos value education highly and view this as a way of rising beyond poverty. Even the daughter's success in some task or school activity is viewed as success for the entire family. [58] Interestingly, *educación* in Latino families not only signifies academic study, but also means politeness and respect for authority. According to Romo, "Schools would do well to capitalize on values related to *familismo* and education to improve the health and education outcomes of Latina girls who are at high risk for negative consequences." [59]

How this translates to the behavior of contemporary Latino youth has a lot to do with the varying level of acculturation to the United States among Hispanic families. Given the sheer diversity of Latino culture, teachers must also understand that some families have assimilated easily into American society, yet, others, particularly new immigrants, have encountered many roadblocks. Sometimes this greatly affects their relationship with the school. [60] Communicating with the school, compounded by a language barrier, can seem threatening to Latino families who have not yet acculturated into American society. On the whole, teachers who remain mindful of the family structure and other cultural values are in a strong position to provide support for Latina girls during the adolescent development.

SUMMARY

The aforementioned review represents only a small part of the literature but hopefully enough to inform teachers, in part, about the identity process of urban adolescents. Given the roller-coaster path of adolescent development, students of color living in poverty encounter a particularly complex web of risk factors. The culture, family structure, urban setting, style of communication, and the challenges of daily living have foundational roles in the identity development of those students sitting in our classroom. Thus, how students socialize and build relationships is rooted in a context very different from those in affluent suburbia.

Teachers, family members, pastors, and other adults, can have an impact on students' lives in spite of risk factors outside the school.[61] According to Ladson-Billings, "When schools support their culture as an integral part of the school experience, students can understand that academic excellence is not the sole province of white middle-class students. Such systems also negate the axiomatic thinking that if doing well in school equals 'acting white' then doing poorly equals 'acting black.'"[62]

The literature consistently reports that teachers play a crucial role in building students' confidence and competence. For that reason, urban teachers must take a difficult but necessary journey to help "young people in developing optimism in the face of hopelessness."[63] Research on Black adolescent males reveals that most of them value education and want to succeed in school but feel unsupported by their teachers.[64] When students are at risk of failing, a teacher's encouragement can mean the difference between passing and failing. Such advocacy impacts students' lives within the school as well as their future goals.[65]

Clearly, urban educators need special reserves of patience for students who require time to develop coping mechanisms for the challenges in their lives. Adjusting internalized habits of behavior happens slowly as students both regress and move forward in tiny steps. From an academic stance, however, patience does not mean passivity or lowering scholastic standards. Ladson-Billings states, "Being aware of the social context is not an excuse for neglecting the classroom tasks associated with helping students to learn literacy, numeracy, scientific, and social skills. Rather it reminds teachers of the larger social purposes of their work."[66]

Unquestionably we need to help adolescents stay in school. Students stay in school when they have an active part of school life. Recommendations from the literature implore educators to provide a diverse range of appealing activities that encourage adolescents to become an active part of the school fabric. We know that students are more likely to stay in school when they form meaningful attachments to friends and teachers. Students also stay in school, according to the research, when they can articulate realistic goals about their schooling and their future.

Critical urban education and informed teaching go hand in hand. To become a critical urban educator, teachers must recognize the value of students' aspirations, strengths, cultural context, and all that makes them the unique special persons that they are. The more in touch we become with aspects that contribute to identity construction in the urban adolescent, the better we can understand how schools can facilitate a place that fosters healthy relationships and pride in academic accomplishment. Urban schools acutely need a cadre of teachers who recognize the sociological, political, and cultural implications of adolescent development. For that reason, encouraging teachers to consider an urban setting goes beyond an idealistic notion of "helping those poor kids" to teaching practice that is both humanistic and informed by thoughtful scholarship.

NOTES

1. Ruben Garza, "Latino and White High School Students' Perception of Caring Behaviors: Are We Culturally Responsive to Our Students?" *Urban Education* 44 (2009): 297. doi: 10.1177/0042085908318714.

2. William Ayers and Ryan Alexander-Tanner, "To Teach: The Journey, in Comics," (lecture, Montclair State University, Upper Montclair, New Jersey, November 5, 2010). This book is a joint collaboration between Ayers as the author and Alexander-Tanner as the illustrator.

3. Patricia B. Kopetz, Anthony J. Lease, and Bonnie Z. Warren-Kring, *Comprehensive Urban Education* (Boston: Pearson, 2006).

4. Katia Goldfarb, "Who Is Included in the Urban Family?" in *19 Urban Questions: Teaching in the City,* ed. Shirley R. Steinberg and Joe L. Kincheloe (New York: Peter Lang, 2007), 261.

5. Shirley R. Steinberg, "What Didn't We Ask: Keepin' It Real," in *19 Urban Questions: Teaching in the City,* ed. Shirley R. Steinberg and Joe L. Kincheloe (New York: Peter Lang, 2007), 282–283.

6. Kopetz, et al., *Comprehensive Urban Education,* 109.

7. Mistlina Sato and Timothy J. Lensmire, "Poverty and Payne: Supporting Teachers to Work with Children of Poverty," *Phi Delta Kappan* 90, no. 5 (2008): 365.

8. Jeanne Theoharis, "I Hate It When People Treat Me Like a Fxxx-up," in *Our Schools Suck,* ed. Gaston Alonso, Noel S. Anderson, Celina Su, and Jeanne Theoharis (New York: New York University Press, 2009), 69–112.

9. See, for example, Russell J. Skiba, Robert S. Michael, Abra Carroll Nardo, and Reece L. Peterson, "The Color of Discipline: Sources of Racial and Gender Disproportionality in School Punishment," *Urban Education* 34, no. 4 (2002): 317–342. doi: 0042-0972/02/1200-0317/0.

10. Suniya S. Luthar, *Poverty and Children's Adjustment,* vol. 41, Developmental Clinical Psychology and Psychiatry Series (Thousand Oaks, CA: Sage Publications, 1999).

11. See, for example, Sato and Lensmire, "Poverty and Payne"; Dena Phillips Swanson, Margaret Beale Spencer, Tabitha Dell'Angelo, Vinay Harpalani, and Tirzah R. Spencer, "Identity Processes and the Positive Youth Development of African Americans: An Explanatory Framework," *New Directions for Youth* 95 (Autumn 2002): 73–99.

12. See, for example, Gaston Alonso, Noel S. Anderson, Celina Su, and Jeanne Theoharis, *Our Schools Suck: Students Talk Back to a Segregated Nation on the Failures of Urban Education* (New York: New York University Press, 2009); Jeffrey M. R. Duncan-Andrade and Ernest Morrell, *The Art of Critical Pedagogy: Possibilities for Moving from Theory to Practice in Urban Schools* (New York: Peter Lang, 2008).

13. See, for example, Alonso, et al., *Our Schools Suck*; Jonathan Kozol, *The Shame of the Nation* (NY: Three Rivers Press, 2005).

14. Richard M. Lerner, Erin Phelps, Amy Alberts, Yulika Forman, and Elise D. Christiansen, "The Many Faces of Urban Girls: Features of Positive Development in Early Adolescence," in *Urban Girls Revisited,* ed. Bonnie J. Ross Leadbeater and Niobe Way (New York: New York University Press, 2007), 22–24.

15. Pedro A. Noguera, *The Trouble With Black Boys: And Other Reflections on Race, Equity, and the Future of Public Education* (San Francisco: Jossey Bass, 2008), 8.

16. See, for example, Beverly D. Tatum, *Why Are All The Black Kids Sitting Together in The Cafeteria?* (New York: Basic Books, 1997).

17. Noguera, *Trouble with Black Boys,* 8.

18. This chapter focuses on Black and Latino ethnicities because they represented the primary racial groups at William Grant Stills High School.

19. Rebecca A. Goldstein, "Who You Think I Am Is Not Necessarily Who I Think I Am," in *Teaching City Kids: Understanding and Appreciating Them,* ed. Joe L. Kincheloe and kecia hayes (New York: Peter Lang, 2007), 105.

20. Swanson, et al., "Identity Processes," 73.

21. LeAlan Jones with David Isay, "From Our America: Life and Death on the South Side of Chicago," in *City Kids, City Schools: More Reports from the Front Row,* ed. William Ayers, Gloria Ladsen-Billings, Gregory Michie, and Pedro A. Noguera (New York: The New Press, 2008), 3.

22. Jones with Isay, "From Our America," 8.

23. Jay P. Greene and Greg Forster, *Public High School Graduation and College Readiness Rates in the United States,* Working Paper, Education, no. 3 (Center for Civic Innovation at the Manhattan Institute, September 2003).

24. R. Duncan-Andrade and Ernest Morrell, *The Art of Critical Pedagogy: Possibilities for Moving from Theory to Practice in Urban Schools* (New York: Peter Lang, 2008), 80.

25. Nilda Flores-González, *School Kids, Street Kids: Identity Development in Latino Students* (New York: Teachers College Press, 2002).

26. Noguera, *Trouble with Black Boys,* (San Francisco, Jossey-Bass, 2008), 142.

27. Mary C. Waters, "The Intersection of Gender, Race, and Ethnicity in Identity Development of Caribbean American Teens," in *Urban Girls: Resisting Stereotypes, Creating Identities,* ed. Bonnie J. Ross Leadbeater and Niobe Way (New York: New York University Press, 1996), 77.

28. John U. Ogbu, "Collective Identity and the Burden of 'Acting White' in Black History, Community and Education," in *Sociology of Education: A Critical Reader,* ed. Alan R. Sadovnik (New York: Routledge, 2007), 305–325.

29. Margaret Beale Spencer, Elizabeth Noll, Jill Stoltzfus, and Vinay Harpalani, "Identity and School Adjustment: Revisiting the 'Acting White' Assumption," *Educational Psychologist* 36, no. 1 (2001): 2–16.

30. Gregory V. Gushue, Christine P. Clark, Karen M. Pantzer, and Kolone R. L. Scanlan, "Self-Efficacy, Perceptions of Barriers, Vocational Identity, and the Career Exploration Behavior of Latino/a High School Students," *The Career Quarterly* 54, no. 4 (2006): 307–317.

31. Luis F. Mirón, "How Do We Locate Resistance in Urban Schools?" in *19 Urban Questions: Teaching in the City,* ed. Shirley R. Steinberg and Joe L. Kincheloe (New York: Peter Lang, 2007), 88.

32. Jennifer Pastor, Jennifer McCormick, and Michelle Fine with Ruth Andolsen, Nora Friedman, Nikki Richardson, Tanzania Roach, and Marina Tavarez, "Makin' Homes: An Urban Girl Thing," in *Urban Girls Revisited,* ed. Bonnie J. Ross Leadbeater and Niobe Way (New York: New York University Press, 2007), 78.

33. Lerner, et al., "The Many Faces of Urban Girls."

34. Noguera, *Trouble with Black Boys,* 142.

35. Swanson, et al., "Identity Processes," 83.

36. Skiba, et al., "The Color of Discipline," 318.

37. Noguera, *Trouble with Black Boys.*

38. Joe L. Kincheloe, "City Kids—Not the Kind of Students You'd Want to Teach," in *Teaching City Kids: Understanding and Appreciating Them,* ed. Joe L. Kincheloe and kecia hayes (New York: Peter Lang, 2007), 13.

39. Noguera, *Trouble with Black Boys,* 22.

40. Swanson, et al., "Identity Processes," 83.

41. Noguera, *Trouble with Black Boys,* 40.

42. Haroon Kharem, "What Does It Mean to Be in a Gang?" in *19 Urban Questions: Teaching in the City,* ed. Shirley R. Steinberg and Joe L. Kincheloe (New York: Peter Lang, 2007), 17.

43. Flores-González, *School Kids, Street Kids,* 128.

44. Elijah Anderson, "The Code of the Streets," *Atlantic Monthly* (May, 1994), 80–94.

45. Bonnie J. Ross Leadbeater and Niobe Way, "Introduction," in *Urban Girls: Resisting Stereotypes, Creating Identities,* ed. Bonnie J. Ross Leadbeater and Niobe Way (New York: New York University Press, 1996), 1; 5.

46. Deborah L. Tolman, "Adolescent Girls' Sexuality: Debunking the Myth of the Urban Girl," in *Urban Girls: Resisting Stereotypes, Creating Identities,* ed. Bonnie J. Ross Leadbeater and Niobe Way (New York: New York University Press, 1996), 256.

47. See, for example, Rosealind Wisman, *Queen Bees and Wannabes: Helping Your Daughter Survive Cliques, Gossip, Boyfriends, and the New Realities of Girl World,* (New York: Three Rivers Press, 2009).

48. Rachel Simmons, *Odd Girl Out* (San Diego: Harcourt, 2002), 3.

49. Beverly Daniel Tatum, *Why Are All the Black Kids Sitting Together in the Cafeteria?* (New York: Basic Books, 1987), 57.

50. Simmons, *Odd Girl Out,* 201.

51. Simmons, *Odd Girl Out,* 225–226.

52. Pastor, et al., "Makin' Homes," 15.

53. Simmons, *Odd Girl Out,* 190; Bianca L. Guzmán, Elise Arruda, and Aida L. Feria, "Los Papas, La Familia y La Sexualidad," in *Latina Girls: Voices of Adolescent Strength in the United States,* ed. Jill Denner and Bianca L. Guzmán (New York: New York University Press, 2006), 17; Marcela Raffaelli and Lenna L. Ontai, "She's 16 Years Old and There's Boys Calling Over to the House: An Exploratory Study of Sexual Socialization in Latino families," *Culture, Health, and Sexuality* 3 (2001): 296; Jill McLean Taylor, "Cultural Stories: Latina and Portuguese Daughters and Mothers," in *Urban Girls: Resisting Stereotypes, Creating Identities,* ed. Bonnie J. Ross Leadbeater and Niobe Way (New York: New York University Press, 1996), 123.

54. Rosealina Diaz, "Latinas in Single Sex Schools," in *Teaching City Kids: Understanding and Appreciating Them,* ed. Joe L. Kincheloe and kecia hayes (New York: Peter Lang, 2007), 4.

55. Jennifer Ayala, "Conianza, Consejos, and Contradictions: Gender and Sexuality Lessons between Latina Adolescent Daughters and Mothers," in *Latina Girls: Voices of Adolescent Strength in the United States,* ed. Jill Denner and Bianca L. Guzmán (New York: New York University Press, 2006), 35.

56. Carlos Salguero and Wendy R. McCusker, "Symptoms Expression in Inner-City Latinas: Psychopathology or Help Seeking?" in *Urban Girls: Resisting Stereotypes, Creating Identities,* ed. Bonnie J. Ross Leadbeater and Niobe Way (New York: New York University Press, 1996), 334.

57. Taylor, "Cultural Stories: Latina and Portuguese Daughters and Mothers," 128.

58. Concha Delgado Gaitan, *Involving Latino Families in Schools: Raising Student Achievement Through Home-School Partnerships* (Thousand Oaks, CA: Corwin Press, 2004), 4.

59. Laura F. Romo, Claudia Kouyoumdjian, Erum Nadeem, and Marian Sigman, "Promoting Values of Education in Latino Mother-Daughter Discussions about Conflict and Sexuality," in *Latina Girls: Voices of Adolescent Strength in the United States,* ed. Jill Denner and Bianca L. Guzmán (New York: New York University Press, 2006), 72.

60. Brunilda DeLeón, "Career Development of Hispanic Adolescent Girls," in *Urban Girls: Resisting Stereotypes, Creating Identities,* ed. Bonnie J. Ross Leadbeater and Niobe Way (New York: New York University Press, 1996), 393–394.

61. See, for example, Swanson, et al., "Identity Processes," 89; Jean E. Rhodes and Anita B. Davis, "Supportive Ties between Nonparent Adults and Urban Adolescent Girls," in *Urban Girls: Resisting Stereotypes, Creating Identities,* ed. Bonnie J. Ross Leadbeater and Niobe Way (New York: New York University Press, 1996), 213.

62. Gloria Ladson-Billings, *The Dreamkeepers: Successful Teachers of African American Children* (San Francisco: Jossey-Bass, 1994), 11.

63. Richard D. Lakes, "Urban Youth and Bibliographic Projects," in *Teaching City Kids: Understanding and Appreciating Them,* ed. Joe L. Kincheloe and kecia hayes (New York: Peter Lang, 2007), 76.

64. Noguera, *Trouble with Black Boys.*

65. See, for example, Kimberly Knesting and Nancy Waldron, "Willing to Play the Game: How At-Risk Students Persist in School," *Psychology in the Schools* 43 (2006): 607. doi: 10.1002/pits.20174; Chandra Muller, "The Role of Caring in the Teacher-Student Relationship for At-Risk Students," *Sociological Inquiry* 71 (2001): 252. http://ejournals.ebsco.com/direct.asp?ArticleID=452DBE32C072D61B00E0.

66. Gloria Ladson-Billings, "Yes, But How Do We Do It?: Practicing Culturally Relevant Pedagogy," in *City Kids, City Schools: More Reports from the Front Row,* ed. William Ayers, Gloria Ladsen-Billings, Gregory Michie, and Pedro A. Noguera (New York: The New Press, 2008), 164.

Chapter Eight

When Students Want to Learn

What do urban students really want from school? Despite what the public may have us believe, urban students do want to learn. Look past the slumped figure, arms crossed at the chest, hood pulled down the forehead, "go-ahead-just-try-to-teach-me" face, and see instead an active, creative mind. Peel through the layers of defensiveness and studied boredom to find a cache of curiosity and wonderment. There is something that makes every teen tick, something that gives way to profound interest, and something that generates excitement about learning.

At WGS, that magic bullet came in the form of an electronic keyboard. Just after the holiday break, fifteen music keyboards were delivered to the school, thanks to the generosity of our partnering university. A new calendar year had unfolded bringing with it opportunities to start over again. The keyboards couldn't have arrived at a better time. Students were fresh and alive from a long week's break and nothing spells excitement like the chance to explore an instrument. Not just any instrument, but one that teens associated with popular music on the radio and music videos.

Music technology may have universal appeal but keyboards need special care if they are to last a long time. Keys can break, headphone wires are prone to tearing, and dropping an instrument causes irreparable damage. Since I traveled from room to room, students needed to set up and put away all the keyboards each music class. Here was an opportunity to teach about care, not just with musical instruments but also with each other. I called it my "Polite Piano Project." The curriculum set goals not just for piano skills but for politeness and civility as well. In other words, I used caring for the keyboard as an "instrument" for addressing caring among the students.

January 8: *Today was our first day with the keyboards. When each student put on his/her pair of earphones the excitement was palpable. Although the room was silent except for the tapping of keys, the students were completely absorbed in their "play" (the task: Find out what this instrument can do). It was impressive. Shakira was dancing in her seat to a demo tape with a huge smile across her face. Marissa kept yelling, "Guys, listen to this," (with her earphones on she had no idea about the volume of her voice).*

Of course some of the students immediately found "porno" sounds or at least that is what they imagined them to be. The "DJ" button was another major hit and many of the students spent their time playing rap-like percussion music. Their delight in the different sound effects was infectious and I found myself running from station to station, laughing out loud at their discoveries.

The smallest successes, like figuring out "Twinkle Twinkle Little Star" or discovering a new sound effect on the keyboard, created a sense of exhilaration that was simply contagious. After the initial class, we began to create sound paintings through various colors and sound effects programmed into the computer. Eventually students wanted to read music. They wanted to play the music they loved such as the theme song from the movie *Titanic*. One student was particularly drawn to the music *Für Elise* (Beethoven), and began to slowly and deliberately to figure out the melody by ear. When others heard the music, they were enchanted.

This prompted my bringing in the movie *Immortal Beloved,* a Hollywood-produced film that captures the very courageous and painful events of Beethoven's life. His story was their story. The abuse that he suffered as a child and the loneliness that enveloped him his whole life spoke directly to their hearts. Even the toughest adolescents found a piece of Beethoven in their lives. His music, thereafter, took on a new poignancy and everyone wanted to play that cool piece, *Für Elise*. The piece itself was way beyond their skill level, but the desire to play it, if only the first few measures of the melody, was a stronger incentive than any kind of external reward. The students were learning because they wanted to.

Reaching that place where students *want* to learn is the ultimate thrill in teaching. It is the point in time where students pull the curriculum forward rather than having the teacher push from behind. Such learning is intrinsically motivated. Because motivation resides in the learner, though, we cannot directly teach motivation just as we cannot make a student learn anything. We can, however, set up conditions that nurture motivated learning.

Daniel and Arapostathis state, "Many times, students who are labeled 'at-risk of academic failure' simply demonstrate a lack of motivation to learn in school."[1] The literature suggests at least three conditions affect motivation: culturally responsive teaching, the ability to tap into students' interests, and the students' perceived relevance of the task.[2] The latter is especially critical because urban students often see the world as having a limited set of possibilities for them. When students do not see a relationship between the learning task and their own lives, instruction based on vague references to what students will need later on in life has little meaning. We know that education can open doors, but initially those doors must have handles that the students can grasp.

The desire to know, in tandem with profound interest, characterizes a highly motivated learning situation. Students need a curriculum that is flexible enough to run with the students' zeal but focused enough to maintain rigorous preparation for participation in a democratic society. Both demand a teacher with breadth and depth of knowledge who is not afraid to adjust the curriculum accordingly.

In the present state of education, however, many teachers feel unfairly constrained by mandated testing assessments. It stands to reason that when scores are used as the sole measure of a teacher's effectiveness, teachers are wary of stepping outside the prescribed boundaries. This concern is real and cannot be ignored.

When a test score defines the net result of schooling, then teachers shift their attention away from the process to the product. Schooling then becomes less about the joy in learning and more about a single measure of achievement. For many teachers, this not only affects their instructional style but also the assessment measures they develop for their students.

The process versus product debate has engulfed educational thought for years, implying that process and product are dichotomous. Yet, both are necessary in evaluating knowledge construction over time. Whereas teaching *to* the test negates the premise of this book, teaching *with* testing criteria in mind summons creative approaches to lessons that not only meet test requirements but provide a rich, student-centered curriculum as well. Once again, good teaching is an intricate matter of balance between process-oriented learning and product-specific outcomes.

The concept of motivation comes into play when teachers genuinely believe that each student wants to learn. Though the student's desire to learn may be hidden under years of denial, there is something that sparks the childlike inquisitiveness within. The challenge in discovering that spark underlies the essence of teaching. "What questions can I ask that will jump-start their interest?" "How can I design a project that will intrigue even the most resistant of my students while still meeting the objectives of this material?"

What motivates one student, however, may not work for another. Ironically, teachers who try to "create" motivation by putting a reward system in place, such as points toward a pizza party or even good grades themselves, work against the very factors that define intrinsically motivated learning. Eventually the rewards are not big enough or novel enough to sustain what appears as excitement in learning. Instead of learning for the pleasure inherent within, students see it as a means to an end.[3] Moreover, adolescents have a keen sense of being conned. Knowing the difference between complicit and voluntary engagement is essential if teachers are committed to authentic learning.[4] While extrinsic rewards may work initially, they do not lead to deeper levels of engagement.

What does engaged learning look like? Although no one can see into the head of his/her student, this type of learning does have visible cues. In engaged learning, students show persistence in solving a problem. They are unlikely to be distracted by other students and intently focus on the problem at hand. Students immersed in problem solving explore a number of different paths (thinking flexibility) in their investigation. Their work is distinguished by growing attentiveness and excitement as pieces fall into place. An engaged student "owns" the problem.[5]

Disengaged learners give up quickly. They show signs of boredom, inattentiveness, and unwillingness to grapple with anything beyond a moderate level of complexity. A problem that is too challenging turns students away. A problem that is too easy demeans what students feel they can do. Teachers skilled in problem-centered instruction, therefore, struggle to design learning problems where students "experience some amounts of frustration without losing them completely to feelings of helplessness."[6]

Perhaps the most challenging type of student is one who is able and intelligent but, for some reason, shows no motivation to participate or complete assignments. Some choose to oppose the school values that they perceive as undermining their self-worth. Others may believe that school achievement is a matter of inborn talents. In other words, abilities are perceived as fixed entities rather than attributable to hard work.

In his study about reluctant learners, Intrator shadowed high school students who described school as listless and dull. He found that students experience time in various ways. These were termed as "flavors of disengagement":[7]

- Slow time: monotonous, predictable, mechanically routine, dull
- Lost time: time unfolds without students being able to describe or articulate any form of experience
- Fake time: students tactically position themselves to appear attentive
- Worry time: time spent worrying about nonacademic matters
- Play time: students seem attentive but remain passive; they may appear to be involved in group work but are actually off task

When students are fully engaged, time is not even a factor. Complete immersion in problem solving renders the concept of time irrelevant, as students seem to lose themselves in process rather than marking time until the class is over.[8]

Projects that involve collaboration provide the teacher with additional clues for observing levels of engagement. The conversations among students as well as how they go about finding a solution become useful indicators. For example, this was particularly evident in a group keyboard project at WGS. The project involved composing a short piece for a chosen scene (i.e., a cave deep in the ocean or the city at rush hour). The following three scenarios illustrate varying levels of engagement in solving this music problem.

- Scenario 1 (high motivation). Peter: "Let's use this sound." Lebrashawn: "What was that thing that Katie did yesterday? Hey Katie, how did you get that weird low sound?" Annie: "Hey guys, listen to this. (She plays an episode on the keyboard). Ginny: "Yeah—that sounds good. We should start with that. It sounds like waves in the ocean." Manny: "Wait, we could turn the volume from loud to soft so it sound like the cave is really far away." The composition begins to evolve as students continue to shape the musical material. The students are goal-oriented and focused on the musicality of the piece.
- Scenario 2 (moderate motivation). Students spend some time trying out different short ideas but lose interest when trying to organize these ideas into a cogent piece of music. Maria: "That sounds stupid." Keneesha: "We have to have something." Tyrone: "Ok, then you just do yours first and then I'll do mine and Keneesha will end it." The final composition was a random collection of ideas rather than a convincing musical piece.
- Scenario 3 (no motivation). Students half-heartedly play a few ideas but eventually lapse into their own conversations. This group did not have a final composition and didn't care. "Reluctant learners," Daniels found, "must find immediate relevance and be truly interested in what they are being taught. Although some students may work if they are not interested to please a teacher or parent, the reluctant learners would not acquiesce so easily."[9]

Although the foregoing scenarios may appear to have little relevance in preparing citizens for a democratic society, the development of engaged, sustained problem solving is central to a healthy democracy. Those sound pieces, for instance, could be the start of a discussion about how artists respond to the world around them because aesthetics are a critical part of the human experience. Teachers can start, then, with small problems that gradually increase in complexity and depth. Helping students develop confidence in their ability to problem solve increases their tolerance for greater complexity and ambiguity.

There are no quick fixes or short-term solutions when it comes to the complexities that underlie a thriving democracy. Most types of productive and lasting changes within a democracy require the ability to work through knotty problems over long periods of time. Students need similar experiences in school. Moreover, students need experience knowing that persistence and deliberation result in worthwhile learning.

Having the commitment to see a problem through implies the ability to delay gratification. Delayed gratification is particularly absent in many of today's adolescents. We live in a society dominated by the need for immediate satisfaction. Fast food restaurants deliver a meal in five minutes, TV provides instant entertainment, and iPods download music faster than the time it takes to listen to the music itself.

Activities such as learning to play an instrument or reading a novel are examples of activities that develop persistence and tenacity. One must engage in these activities for some length of time in order to experience the reward of the journey. Although there is no difference among teens regarding the capacity for intrinsic motivation, adolescents from affluent circumstances have far more opportunities to explore "adventuresome" activities than disadvantaged teens. [10]

Impoverished students, for instance, lack the money for summer camp, travel, or after-school activities such as participation on a hockey team. Consequently, there are fewer alternatives to discover areas of interest that may result in long-term engagement. Such a context mitigates self-learning and the kind of stimulating exchange that nurtures different ways of seeing the world.

Teaching in an urban setting, therefore, relies on sensitivity to the context in which students live. When families can only concentrate on getting by one day at a time, there is little time for developing self-sustained interests beyond attending to basic needs. In addition, a society that promotes faster as better yields fewer opportunities for developing patience and persistence. This does not mean that students cannot develop those dispositions, but it does mean that teachers need to understand their social framework in order to nurture increased focus on the task.

The students at WGS did not need any coaxing to start playing the keyboard. Its social relevance and technological intrigue was already a high motivator. How to maintain that strong interest, though, became the greater challenge.

Initially, students felt competent in exploring the keyboard; they only needed to push buttons or keys to create sound—no previous skill was needed nor were any of the students particularly skilled in keyboard playing. From that perspective it was a relatively even playing field. When students wanted to play songs, however, they realized that they needed either a very good ear (the ability to hear a melody and translate it to the keyboard) or had to learn music notation. The motivation to learn music reading was high because they had a desire to move forward with their skills.

Reading music is a skill that some developed quickly and others very slowly. To account for these differences, reading activities were differentiated from simply reading the alphabet letter of the note name, "E," to reading that same note on the staff without help. Later on, students could choose their own pieces from repertoires that ranged from low ability to high ability. Although the tasks were differentiated by ability, the students did not necessarily choose songs that I thought matched their ability; I also never specified, to the students, which songs were more difficult than others. This turned out as a blessing in disguise because just wanting to play a certain piece compelled students to take a giant leap in their skills.

The final project was to play a solo piece in a class recital. Some students managed a one-hand melody while other students were able to also play a simple bass line accompaniment. The recital was staged for guests (teachers on break, school coordinator, the university liaison, etc.) and the students were asked to dress according to the occasion. In addition, students were taught basic performance etiquette such as polite audience behavior, how to bow at the end of the piece, and how to behave in a receiving line.

During the recital it was heartwarming to see students supporting their classmates and responding with wild applause as each took his/her turn at the piano. Some of the toughest students had shaking hands when they sat down but showed great determination to play from start to finish. All of the students approached the recital with appropriate seriousness, wanting their friends to do well. It seems that the caring part of the curriculum was a strong as the skills learned.

Teaching, then, involves more than content. It necessitates a conscious realization that students need to learn how to work at something over a period of time without giving up. It also means that teachers may have to teach for patience and self-control. One cannot assume that these are natural outgrowths of school work or that some students have it and others do not.

Conceptualizing teaching from this standpoint broadens the role of the teacher. Whereas most teachers think about curriculum in terms of what, how, and when to teach content, the process of learning to learn demands a similar conscious awareness. Questions like "How far should I go in the textbook to cover the area of Chinese culture?" ought to change into questions like "What projects or problem-solving activities can I design that will teach Chinese culture but also stimulate sustained interest?"

Persistence in problem solving, confidence in one's ability to persevere, and task complexity are woven from the same cloth. Each depends upon the other two for substantive learning to take place. Moreover, there is no prescribed formula for accomplishing this as students not only have different learning styles but different levels of motivation as well.

Good teachers are, by nature, tenacious and used to dealing with multi-level tasks. Their teaching goals are rooted in essential questions of the discipline and their approach to instruction takes into account the many ways in which students learn. They develop stratified projects—students can choose from a variety of formats for demonstrating their knowledge—that encourage autonomy and control.[11] Using the Chinese culture example above, students might show their understanding with a diary entry through the eyes of a farmer, a PowerPoint presentation, an informative brochure, or performing/presenting some area of Chinese art.

On the other hand, experienced teachers or novice teachers cannot strategically nudge students forward without having had personal experience with challenging problems. For teachers, the challenge is to move from the experiential level to pedagogical practice. That is, teachers need to make the connection between their own experiences with complex problem solving and planning to similar experiences for their students. Only then can teachers truly understand the reasons for presenting tasks that challenge, frustrate, but ultimately result in gratifying learning gains.

Likewise, teacher educators must help pre-service teachers translate personal experiences to relevant practice in the field. Novice teachers need two things: (a) a cognitive understanding of the reasons for engaging students in problem solving, and (b) the assurance that some level of frustration is a necessary part of the process. Adkins also comments, "Pre-service teachers need concrete pictures of what facilitating engagement looks like in practice to be ready to accept the challenges of urban teaching."[12] When such experiences are built into the teacher education program, pre-service students can learn valuable lessons about cognitive and affective dimensions of the learning process.

If teachers can create opportunities that trigger the *need to know*, students will pursue a solution on their own. Sustaining interest is the teacher's biggest challenge for genuine learning to take place. When teachers can develop problems that increase in complexity but are diverse enough to allow access for every student, they are truly reflecting teaching as an art form. This kind of teaching is not a consequence of years of experience but a subtle combination of knowing the student, sensing how much to push the student, recognizing that frustration is a necessary part of growing, and celebrating the outcomes as real, authentic learning that is but part of the larger cycle of acquiring knowledge.

The evolution of a democracy depends on citizens who are intrinsically motivated to bring about change, especially with issues of social justice. Not all content directly lends itself to issues of social justice, but there is the possibility in every subject area to develop problem-solving skills, purposefulness, and tenacity.

From a democratic standpoint, preparing students to think intelligently and independently within a social context contributes to meaningful decisions that affect our society. If we agree that these are the kinds of citizens that forward the common good, then schooling must teach both for content and for the dispositions that drive stewardship.

The "need to know" is an impulse that emanates from the student. The artist teacher taps into that initial impulse and flies with it. Teachers begin to uncover latent curiosity by asking questions that provoke critical thinking and posing problems that do not always have clear solutions. The more students become engaged in learning, the greater their tolerance for complex problem solving.[13] Along with this comes an increase in persistence, tenacity, and confidence in one's ability to work through difficult problems.

We have to believe that great possibilities exist in each student. Without such conviction, teachers continue to follow their familiar mechanized routines in planning and teaching the lesson. Teachers who delight in their content and novel ways of engaging students, however, not only inspire reticent students but also keep that spark glowing. It is this inner glow that reminds teachers why they went into teaching in the first place.

NOTES

1. Erika Daniels and Mark Arapostathis, "What Do They Really Want?: Student Voices and Motivation Research," *Urban Education* 40 (2006): 231. doi: 10.1177/0042085904270421.

2. Theresa A. Adkins-Coleman, "I'm Not Afraid to Come into Your World: Case Studies of Teachers Facilitating Engagement in Urban High School English Classrooms," *The Journal of Negro Education* 79, no. 1 (2010): 41.

3. Daniels and Arapostathis, "What Do They Really Want?"

4. Committee on Increasing High School Students' Engagement and Motivation to Learn and National Research Council, "The Nature and Conditions of Engagement," in *Engaging Schools: Fostering High School Students' Motivation to Learn* (Washington, DC: The National Academies Press, 2003).

5. Lisa C. DeLorenzo, "A Field Study of Sixth-Grade Students' Creative Music Problem-Solving Processes," *Journal of Research in Music Education* 37 (1989): 188–200. doi: 10.2307/3344669.

6. Daniels and Arapostathis, "What Do They Really Want?" 49.

7. Sam Instrator, "The Engaged Classroom," *Educational Leadership* 62 (2004): 2.

8. See, for example, Mihaly Csikszentmihalyi, *Flow: The Psychology of Optimal Experience* (New York: Harper and Row, 1990).

9. Daniels and Arapostathis, "What Do They Really Want?" 55.

10. Florence C. Ladd, "City Kids in the Absence of . . ." in *Children, Nature, and the Urban Environment: Proceedings of a Symposium-Fair;* Gen. Tech. REP. NE-30 (Upper Darby: U.S. Department of Agriculture, Forest Service, Northeastern Forest Experiment Station, 1977), 76–81.

11. Matthew J. Dicento and Sandra Gee, "Control is the Key: Unlocking the Motivation of At-Risk Students," *Psychology in the Schools* 36, no. 3 (1999): 231–237.

12. Adkins-Coleman, "I'm Not Afraid to Come into Your World," 51.

13. Allan Wigfield, Jacquelynne S. Eccles, and Daniel Rodriguez, "The Development of Children's Motivation in School Contexts," in *Review of Research in Education,* ed. A. Iran-Nejad and P. D. Pearson, vol. 23 (Washington, DC: American Educational Research Association, 1998).

Chapter Nine

White Teachers, Urban Schools

> How much does it matter if a child cannot identify ethnically or racially with a teacher? Does it matter at all? If the teacher accepts him and likes him as he really is, isn't that enough?
>
> —Vivian Gussin Paley, *White Teacher*[1]

It is daunting for White teachers to teach students of a different race. Unless teachers have fooled themselves into believing that "kids are kids" or "I don't see color," White teachers have a huge chasm to traverse in order to truly understand each child for who he/she is. Ignoring color is to ignore identity. Ignoring identity is tantamount to rendering a child invisible. Those of us who are White teachers and who somewhat understand the complexities of race recognize that our frame of reference lies far outside that of the children of color in our classrooms. The question "Who are you?" that often comes first is not reasonable without asking, "Who am I?"

White persons, in general, have a difficult time defining themselves in terms of race. True introspection of one's self as White means confronting the misnomer that White sets the standard or norm of American society, resulting in an "us" and "them" dichotomy instead of "we." To move beyond this line of demarcation, Whites must come face to face with the fact that in some way they have contributed to a society that does not afford equality to every citizen. In short, the term democracy does not mean the same thing to all citizens.

A frank discussion of race, as it affects schooling and those who are schooled, raises many troubling issues. Many are uncomfortable with the realization that society benefits some more than others. We are further appalled to find that schools, like other American institutions, continue to engage in practices that disadvantage certain students on the basis of skin color. Although social class, economic status, and gender are often intertwined with race, issues of race can be scrutinized without these other factors.

For White teachers, it is important to walk through the looking glass and examine ourselves and the students that we teach. Whereas teachers of color have personal experience with racism, White teachers have the least experience with institutionalized racism. Yet, White teachers comprise the bulk of the teaching force. This provides a powerful argument for addressing race in teacher education. In our increasingly diverse classrooms, White teachers have an acute need to examine their racial biases and stereotypical thinking.

At WGS, my students were primarily Black and Latino but I also had a few students of Indian descent, Chinese descent, Middle Eastern descent, and one White student. The Black and Latino students, however, were most vocal about their racial identity. These students talked openly and often about race, something that surprised me as a White person who grew up in a community where race was not discussed. Although their candor was audacious at times, it was remarkable to watch these adolescents deal head on with the raw issues of race and racist behavior.

> March 5: *I can't shake the guilt that I feel as a White teacher among students of color. Though they never confronted me about race, I worry that they secretly despise the fact that I am White. I realize that, by virtue of my color, I am in the dominant social circle and, in fact, am part of a greater scheme that oppresses the families of my students. I want to say that I am sorry—sorry that I am White—sorry that our faculty structure is primarily White—sorry that I will never fully know what it feels like to bear the burden of color in our society.*

Guilt is not an unusual feeling for White persons struggling to understand their place in a racist society. Many, however, would defiantly deny that we live in a racist society. In her early struggle to confront racial feelings, Peggy McIntosh writes, "I did not see myself as a racist because I was taught to recognize racism only in individual acts of meanness by members of my group, never in invisible systems conferring unsought racial dominance on my group from birth."[2] As McIntosh intimates, we try to exclude ourselves from the term "racist," because we often associate racism only with particular acts of aggression against a person or persons of color.

Because "racism" is emotionally loaded, it is helpful to understand what scholars mean by the term race. The literature portrays race as a social construct. Hyland states, "I understand race as a historically and socially assigned category. That is, one's race is not biologically determined; rather, it is socially constructed as a result of history, politics, and economics."[3] Racial bigotry refers to individual intolerance of persons of color, while institutional racism is something that permeates the social structure by denying persons respect, resources, or opportunities. "White racism refers to something more powerful than individual acts of bigotry, although such acts are related to racism in significant ways. Institutional racism, in the United States, is a system—supported by discourse, ideology, the legal system, and everyday practice—that perpetuates White dominance."[4]

The idea of institutional racism, however, is difficult for Whites to accept because it holds us accountable for participating in practices that subordinate persons of color. In other words, when we accept the status quo or refuse to acknowledge that acts of racism are inherent in American society, we sustain a racist public. How does this filter into the arts?

Consider, for example, a seemingly benign question about orchestras. Why are there so few Black musicians in premiere American orchestras? The question is tangentially relevant to public education because most students have their first formalized music class in school. My contention is that given the lack of arts resources in many urban schools and the money it takes to support a young musician, most urban students don't have a chance of entertaining thoughts about a professional music career (including music teaching). While cutbacks in the arts are also making it more and more difficult for students in suburban and rural areas, the state of affairs in an urban setting is far deeper.

Let's explore the path of a student who majors in music at a college, conservatory, or university. Many children get a start in elementary school, sometimes as young as preschool. In adolescence, talented students who might have an orchestral career begin to play in prestigious youth orchestras or are accepted in well-known pre-college music programs such as the Juilliard School or North Carolina School of the Arts. The private artist teacher, who charges upwards of sixty or more dollars per hour, is a critical piece in the music training process because he/she mentors the student in terms of summer music programs, competitions, and connections with other artists. At some point, serious music students need to purchase an instrument at a cost that would be prohibitive to impoverished youth. They attend concerts on a regular basis and perform often.

It should be noted that some artists make it in the professional music world despite these challenges. Nevertheless, these musicians are exceptions to the rule. Ultimately, the path to a professional career in music is long, expensive, and often dependent on the private teacher's connections with other artists.

Other disciplines do not require such extensive training but, instead, pose questions of curriculum. When the teaching of American history, for instance, does not fully represent the contributions of racial and ethnic groups in the advancement of our society, students of color are denied an authentic portrait of American life. The same example rings true for other disciplines, especially in the arts and language arts.

In terms of tracking, it is no secret that primarily White students populate the higher-level classes, including advanced placement courses. Part of the problem rests with educators who do not encourage students of color to take advanced placement courses. The very inference that students of color are less capable than Whites reflects a deeply hidden and often subconscious belief that Whites are superior over persons of color.

Decisions that deny Black or Latino students the same academic opportunities as other students may seem insignificant on a classroom level. Yet, it is imperative to recognize that such decisions seep like a toxin through the entire educational system. This kind of institutional racism not only affects access to upper-level courses but also affects career opportunities and status in the larger society.

Even the language that we expect and accept from our students reflects a Eurocentric standard. In the book *The Skin That We Speak,*[5] various authors discuss ways in which White teachers may unwittingly reject the student's culture and cultural background. "It is almost impossible," Stubbs explains, "to hear someone speak without immediately drawing conclusions, possibly very accurate, about his social class background, level of education, and what part of the country he comes from."[6] The problem is not so much the identification of these indices as much as it is in the value judgments that guide us to label certain students as "dumb," "poor readers," or "speech impaired."[7]

All people experience discrimination at some point in their lives, whether it involves religion, sexual orientation, gender, disability, or even body weight. And while this is not quite the same as institutionalized racism, it is a portal through which teachers can begin to examine their feelings of "otherness." The discomfort that accompanies reflection of this sort is particularly painful. Self-examination for racial bias, paradoxically, can work well in a group setting such as professional development workshops, where teachers have an opportunity to hear diverse perspectives.

In examining racial discrimination, Whites learn to bury their feelings because talking about it is seen either as impolite or politically incorrect.[8] Tatum writes, "many Whites have been encouraged by their culture of silence to disconnect from their racial experiences."[9] We don't want to admit to ourselves or to our friends of color that we sometimes form a negative perspective on Blacks and Latinos through stereotypical thinking.

One technique for opening the door to conversations about race is to explore what it means to be White. For teachers who have never thought about themselves as "White," this first step is highly personal and often threatening. When people feel threatened, they often become extremely defensive, "Some of my best friends are Black" or "I don't harbor prejudices against people of color because I was brought up to believe that we are all equal."

LeCompte and McCray examined the racial awareness of White teacher education students, and revealed that individual guilt and anger emerged first. A common response goes something like this: "My grandparents immigrated from Poland but they worked hard and made a good life for themselves. *These* (i.e., Black) *people* just need to pull themselves up by their bootstraps and contribute to society."[10] In other words, "most Americans analyze who gets what only in terms of individual effort and ability."[11]

This kind of thinking supports the concept of meritocracy—that if you work hard enough, you will rise on the socio-economic ladder. To refute this argument means to accept that our democracy is not a "relatively open system that emphasizes individual choice and mobility."[12] Discussions of this nature often include the term "White privilege."

White privilege—the recognition that Whites are born with social and economic advantages simply because of skin color—is the terminology used most often to help White persons understand the underlying tentacles of racism. According to Hyland, "Racism is not a problem for people simply because they are White, but because they were raised within a system and context that normalizes racial grouping and has educated them to a worldview that assumes that Whiteness is superior."[13] Such a dramatic realization is, for most White teachers, shocking and unnerving, for it turns one's long-held beliefs upside down.

March 9: *I never realized how systemic racism is infused in contemporary society until a graduate student of mine spoke about his own experience with racial discrimination. A well-respected high school teacher living in an affluent suburb, Mr. B. talked about the many times he was pulled over to the side of the road without having committed a driving offense. One time he came into class visibly shaken. The bank refused to cash his paycheck until they had completed a tedious evaluation of his financial status. Would a White man undergo this kind of scrutiny for such a routine activity? Probably not. It hurt to see this soft-spoken Black man subject to investigations that I had never experienced nor probably would experience in my lifetime. How could I be so naïve as to think that racism ended with the civil rights movement?*

Howard writes that "honesty begins for Whites when we learn to question our own assumptions and acknowledge the limitations of our culturally conditioned perceptions of the truth."[14] No conversation could be more critical than that in the schools. The truth is, our schools perpetuate inequality, for example, when some students receive considerably more resources than others . . . when the cost per student is significantly lower in some schools than others, and so on. The ramifications of these conditions speak to a truth that hits too close to home.

Good teachers are especially sensitive to fairness. They struggle through-out their careers to establish rules of behavior, inclusive teaching practice, and assessment strategies that reflect a sense of equity in the way they work with their students. For this reason, the very thought of living in a society in which fairness is called into question strikes discord in the teacher's heart.

Although we cannot fix the complex nature of racism in our society, we can take an active role in identifying and counteracting racist behavior or practice in the school. It takes courage to openly discuss race and racism in the classroom or in the faculty room. Silence or neutrality, while seemingly more comfortable, sustains an environment of White domination. [15] The price we pay for our silence results in prolonging the myth that some students are inherently more deserving than others.

When are we confronted with racially tinged situations? Some of the issues happen right in front of our faces: a student utters a racial slur or a faculty member tells a racist joke. Whether shrouded in comedy or malice, teachers must confront the behavior rather than pretend it never happened, or constantly dismiss the behavior as "That wasn't nice" or "We don't tolerate that kind of remark here." The latter may seem effective, but in reality, never teaches the offender or the audience why racial remarks are serious affronts to a person's culture.

Finding the right words to say at the right time is the heart of the matter. Racial remarks do not happen at convenient times, nor should we assume that these situations always involve Whites and students of color. It is sometimes the case that students of color insult those within their own race.

> April 10: *Eva emigrated from West Africa and is one of my favorite students. She is so capable with such a beautiful smile. Though very quiet, she has a spirit of generosity toward other students and is always willing to help. I wonder why she seems to have only one friend? Shawna answered this without my asking: "Nobody likes that Eva. She is too black." Shawna was referring to the shade of her skin. I couldn't believe it. One Black student criticizing another Black student for the color of her skin . . . where is this coming from?*

Racial bias within the same race is disturbing but should not sidetrack us from acknowledging racist language among any of our students. Addressing such language or related incidents need not take the form of an attack. One can talk about racist remarks in terms of their effect on all students, not just the victims of the remark or joke. It is important that we openly discuss stereotyping and slurs as examples of putting people down and disrespecting their culture.

While no approach is failsafe, there are a few ways in which teachers might address an incidence that is racial in nature. One can take a student aside for a nonconfrontational conversation about the impact that his/her remarks have on others. Sometimes, however, the situation is such that calling attention to the remark or attitude would create more damage to the injured person, simply because the student might feel even more targeted. In these situations, teachers may choose to talk about racist remarks at a time that is removed from the incident.

On the other hand, a teacher might approach the situation obliquely through the context of a story or content studied in class (e.g., the story of Rosa Parks). This idea is only useful if it provides a bridge for talking about racism in students' everyday lives. Students do not always realize the effect that their speech has on others. Because we are responsible for creating a safe learning environment, students must understand that offhand remarks can hurt despite the fact that targeted students may laugh or show no observable offense.

In terms of colleagues, there is often a power differential that makes it very difficult or impossible to address racist language/behavior. In fact, Tatum states that "well-intentioned white middle/upper middle class teachers can publicly condemn racism and class bias while unconsciously engaging in behaviors that perpetuate structural forms of these social pathologies."[16] If speaking privately with the person is not an option, it may help to request professional development workshops with clinicians skilled in working with racist attitudes and behavior.

Hidden forms of racism and White dominance in the schools are more difficult to recognize. "Teacher's attitudes and perceptions," remarks Mozzei, "are not always revealed in what they say" but rather how and what they teach.[17] White teachers are so steeped in a history that focuses on White representation and decision making, that a curriculum which furthers this perspective unconsciously verifies what White teachers know to be true.

Token references via holidays (e.g., Martin Luther King Day or Chinese New Year) do not substitute for a culturally responsive curriculum. Nor does it make much difference to discuss books by authors of color without talking about the racial/cultural context. Yet White teachers who have worked in other cultures can also inform our thinking. Bobby Starnes taught on the Chippewa-Cree reservation in northern Montana for several years.[18] Her reflection as a White teacher in a Native American culture lends an intriguing perspective to issues of race and schooling. She found that teachers cannot fully teach children of another culture without knowing their history, culture, or community. "In such cases, solid teaching skills, good intentions, hard work, and loving kids just aren't enough."[19]

Her notes to White teachers are worth considering:[20]

- Find mentors (in the culture)—it is important to work closely with a mentor to ensure that what we do is both correct and appropriate
- Get educated
- Know and participate in the community

- Question personal knowledge of historical "facts"
- Expect measured success—Success will not be immediate or consistent
- Push for training—better teacher preparation

The last note, push for better teacher preparation, is crucial for developing a cadre of teachers who are sensitive to their own prejudices and biases. Because most teacher education students are White and receive instruction from White teacher educators, courageous conversations about race must take place in the university classroom. Although many teacher education institutions provide urban field experiences, without accompanying dialogue and reflection beginning teachers are likely to maintain an "us versus them" perspective. [21]

Most pre-service teachers tend to think of themselves as "prejudice free" and giving "fair treatment to all despite skin color." [22] Challenging White pre-service and in-service teachers to think about themselves as a race that is not only dominant in America but also privileged does not happen easily or comfortably. [23] People do not quickly give up their long-felt values or beliefs. For this reason, one must recognize that the process of changing perspective is both gradual and emotionally laden. One or two university classes or in-service workshops are but the beginning of a difficult journey.

Hill-Jackson found that White pre-service teachers go through stages in shifting their multi-cultural perspective. [24] In the beginning stages, teachers are often oblivious to the fact that others see the world differently from themselves. They perceive racism as individual acts against other persons and believe in the cause-effect nature of life: "Whites get higher grades than Blacks because White families have more support for education."

Once White teachers become increasingly aware of other cultures and their differing perspectives of life, there is anger, frustration, and guilt. These feelings arise from sheer cognitive dissonance that accompanies any process where individuals confront their deeply held beliefs and values. Hill-Jackson terms this stage as "multicultural purgatory" [25] where an individual wrestles with reconciling old ways of thinking and assimilating new information. If not treated with care, strong emotions can shut down the hard work of examining one's beliefs and the individual recedes back to his/her comfort zone.

At best, individuals reach a stage of critical consciousness where they have examined and identified their own biases in the context of a multicultural world. Critical consciousness reflects the ability to recognize the barriers that ethnic groups encounter and the role in which Whites contribute to those barriers. A Eurocentric vision of the world is replaced with an understanding that many voices need equal access to the democratic process. Efforts to reach a stage of critical consciousness are crucial not just in teacher preparation but for all teachers as well. According to Delpit, "Until we can see the world as others see it, all the educational reforms in the world will come to naught."[26]

> March 15: *I will never fully know what it is like to be Black or Latino. I understand that the color of my skin affords me many advantages and I recognize that I don't do enough to celebrate the contributions of Black and Latino racial groups. Their musical culture is rich, yet I am not doing enough to celebrate the musical heritage of students of color. As I think about it, I wonder if I am afraid—afraid to teach something for which I have no first-hand, living experience.*

This journal entry brings to light some of the basic questions that I have struggled with through my teaching experience: Would my students respect me more if I were Black or Latino? Do I, as a White teacher, have validity among students of color or do I represent the legions of White people who have and continue to dominate our society? In my students' eyes, does my skin color negatively set me apart from my colleagues of color?

The questions are genuine but the implication is troubling: that students learn best from teachers of their own race. If so, then the ideals of democracy and its roots firmly planted in pluralism have no meaning. Paley writes, "Homogeneity is fine in a bottle of milk, but in the classroom it diminishes the curiosity that ignites discovery."[27] The wisdom of her words suggests that diversity is a blessing, not an obstacle. White teachers have much to offer Black/Latino children and Black/Latino teachers have much to offer White children. The same also holds true for teachers and students of other races and cultures.

In a recent conversation with a group of ninth grade African American students, I asked students whether they feel a different kind of connection with a Black teacher versus a White teacher. Their answers were intriguing:

> We want teachers who care about us, give us challenging work, and never give up on us. Sometimes a Black teacher just knows where we're coming from but this does not affect how we look at teachers in general. The color of the teacher is not important. What is important is that the teacher works with us, treats us as adults and also plays around with us (harmless joking). We just want to learn things. We like it when we get different perspectives from different kinds of teachers.

We cannot teach if we are burdened by political correctness or shame from our Whiteness. Sometimes the fear of a racist label can paralyze teachers into shirking their leadership role so as not to appear oppressive. As a result, classrooms lack structure and discipline under the guise of being "non-oppressive and democratic."[28] Consequently, teachers tend to avoid conversations about race with their students and colleagues.

Our role, as White teachers, is to create an empathic environment where students have the freedom to speak about racism in a meaningful way and where academic judgments are made with the best interests of the child at heart. In terms of stewardship, it is important that White teachers develop a critical consciousness about race and actively seek to eliminate racism in curriculum, school policies, and student/faculty conversations. The goal of White educators is to become "personally conscious" as educators committed to "social healing and positive change."[29]

Democratic practice in the schools compels us to question policies and behaviors that advantage one race over another. In my personal experience, such an example occurred several years ago: a neighboring school district continued to keep the school open on Martin Luther King Day, while most other districts were closed. Students who were African American were granted an excused absence if they chose to participate in out-of-school activities; however, in the end, they would miss all their classes.

While African American students appeared to have a choice, in reality there was no choice. Moreover, it sent a clear message to other students that Martin Luther King and his contributions to American society did not warrant special attention. Concerned teachers in this mostly White district openly challenged the policy. As a result of well-crafted arguments and numerous complaints, the school district ultimately changed its policy and closed the schools on Martin Luther King Day.

When White teachers truly understand that there are many lenses from which to view the world, they are in a position to appreciate the differences that make each child remarkable. "If teachers pretend not to see students' racial and ethnic differences," Laddson-Billings writes, "they really do not see the students at all and are limited in their ability to meet their educational needs."[30] Silence is our worst enemy. By remaining silent, we tacitly condone a system that is inherently flawed and undemocratic. By intertwining race with other of areas of disadvantage, such as class or gender, we diminish the role that race plays in enriching social relationships and enhancing learning experiences.

At the beginning of this chapter, Vivian Paley asks whether it is enough to accept and like a student as he/she really is. I would respectfully add that celebrating a child for who himself/herself is is but one part of the discussion. We need teachers who are not only true to themselves but also question how and what the child is taught. In addition, we need teachers who passionately believe that color-blindness denies the rights of all children to embrace and appreciate the multiple ways of viewing our world. Such attitudes and values undergird endeavors to sustain genuine democratic practice in the schools.

NOTES

1. Vivian Gussin Paley, *White Teacher* (Cambridge, MA: Harvard University Press, 1979), 35.

2. Peggy McIntosh, "White Privilege: Unpacking the Invisible Knapsack," *Peace and Freedom Magazine* (July/August 1989): 4–5.

3. Nora E. Hyland, "Being a Good Teacher of Black Students? White Teachers and Unintentional Racism," *Curriculum Inquiry* 35 (2005): 431.

4. Hyland, "Being a Good Teacher," 431.

5. Lisa Delpit and Joanne K. Dowdy, eds., *The Skin That We Speak: Thoughts on Language and Culture in the Classroom* (New York: The New Press, 2008).

6. Michael Stubbs, "Some Basic Sociolinguistic Concepts," in *The Skin That We Speak,* ed. Lisa Delpit and Joanne K. Dowdy (New York: The New Press, 2008), 66.

7. Asa G. Hilliard III, "Language, Culture, and the Assessment of African American Children," in *The Skin That We Speak,* ed. Lisa Delpit and Joanne K. Dowdy (New York: The New Press, 2008), 9.

8. Lisa A. Mozzei, "Silence Speaks: Whiteness Revealed in the Absence of Voice," *Teaching and Teacher Education* 24, (2008): 1125–1136.

9. Beverly Daniel Tatum, *Why Are All the Black Kids Sitting Together in the Cafeteria?* (New York: Basic Books, 1987), 201.

10. Karen Nicol LeCompte and Audren Davis McCray, "Complex Conversations with Teacher Candidates: Perspectives of Whiteness and Culturally Responsive Teaching," *Curriculum and Teaching Dialogue* 4 (2002): 25–35.

11. Enid Lee, "Anti-Racist: Pulling Together to Close the Gaps," in *Beyond Heroes and Holidays: A Practical Guide to K–12 Anti-Racist, Multicultural Education and Staff Development,* ed. Enid Lee, Deborah Menkart, and Margo Okazawa-Rey (Washington, DC: Network of Educators on the Americas, 1998), 3.

12. Christine Sleeter, "Teaching Whites About Racism," in *Beyond Heroes and Holidays: A Practical Guide to K–12 Anti-Racist, Multicultural Education and Staff Development,* ed. Enid Lee, Deborah Menkart, and Margo Okazawa-Rey (Washington, DC: Network of Educators on the Americas, 1998), 37.

13. Hyland, "Being a Good Teacher," 432.

14. Gary R. Howard, *We Can't Teach What We Don't Know: White Teachers, Multiracial Schools* (New York: Teachers College Press, 1999), 69.

15. See, for example, Rita Kohli, "Critical Race Reflections: Valuing the Experiences of Teachers of Color in Teacher Education," *Race, Ethnicity and Education* 12, no. 2 (2009): 235–251; Mozzei, "Silence Speaks"; and Tatum, *Why Are All The Black Kids Sitting Together in the Cafeteria?*

16. Joe L. Kincheloe, "City Kids—Not the Kind of Students You'd Want to Teach," in *Teaching City Kids: Understanding and Appreciating Them,* ed. Joe L. Kincheloe and kecia hayes (New York: Peter Lang, 2007), 9.

17. Mozzei, "Silence Speaks," 1129.

18. Bobby Ann Starnes, "What We Don't Know Can Hurt Them: White Teachers, Indian Children," *Phi Delta Kappan* 87 (2006), 384–392.

19. Starnes, "What We Don't Know," 358.

20. Starnes, "What We Don't Know," 390.

21. Caryn Terwilliger, "Mapping Stories: Taking Detours to Challenge Whiteness," *Making Connections: Interdisciplinary Approaches to Cultural Diversity* 11 (2010): 14–25.

22. Sandra M. Lawrence and Beverly Daniel Tatum, "White Racial Identity and Anti-Racist Education: A Catalyst for Change," in *Beyond Heroes and Holidays: A Practical Guide to K–12 Anti-Racist, Multicultural Education and Staff Development,* ed. Enid Lee, Deborah Menkart, and Margo Okazawa-Rey (Washington, DC: Network of Educators on the Americas, 1998), 48.

23. See, for example, Valerie A. Middleton, "Increasing Preservice Teachers' Diversity Beliefs and Commitment," *Urban Review,* 34 (2002): 343–361; Sandra M. Lawrence and Beverly Daniel Tatum, "White Racial Identity and Anti-Racist Education: A Catalyst for Change" in *Beyond Heroes and Holidays: A Practical Guide to K–12 Anti-Racist, Multicultural Education and Staff Development,* ed. Enid Lee, Deborah Menkart, and Margo Okazawa-Rey (Washington, DC: Network of Educators on the Americas, 1998), 48–55.

24. Valerie Hill-Jackson, "Wrestling Whiteness: Three Stages of Shifting Multicultural Perspectives Among White Pre-Service Teachers," *Multicultural Perspectives* 9 (2007): 29–35. doi: 10.1080/15210960701386285.

25. Hill-Jackson, "Wrestling Whiteness."

26. Lisa Delpit, *Other People's Children* (New York: The New Press, 2006), 134.

27. Paley, *White Teacher,* 56.

28. Jeffrey M. R. Duncan-Andrade and Ernest Morrell, *The Art of Critical Pedagogy: Possibilities for Moving from Theory to Practice in Urban Schools* (New York: Peter Lang, 2008), 179.

29. Howard, *We Can't Teach What We Don't Know,* 6.

30. Gloria Ladson-Billings, *The Dreamkeepers: Successful Teachers of African American Children* (San Francisco: Jossey-Bass, 1994), 33.

Chapter Ten

The Democratic School: Is It Worth It?

For those who believe in democratic schools and, consequently, take action to initiate or preserve democratic practice, the challenges are akin to finding a needle in a haystack. According to Soder, "We need to understand that it is often more difficult to sustain a democracy than it is to create it."[1] Surely, the authoritarian top-down governance model found in so many schools today is not only easier to implement but also to maintain. The question then becomes, "Is it worth it?" Or as Soder shockingly asks, "Democracy—do we really want it?"[2]

Perhaps our rhetoric has become so complacent that we have ceased to carefully examine what democracy means and what it demands of its citizens. Because democracy is an ever-evolving construct, it requires "continuous examination in light of changing times."[3] Such philosophical probing of democracy is necessary, however, as it raises the precarious question, "Why democracy in our schools?"

Most people immediately link democracy with a political model. The connection is understandable; voting for public office, engaging in legislation by and for the people, or even going to war with other countries based on the premise that democracy is a moral right, fills our news headlines on a daily basis. The relationship of politics and democracy, in America, is a loud, unremitting voice.

With this in mind, teachers who wish to democratize their classrooms tend to focus on issues of structure. These issues include students and teachers developing classroom rules, designing project rubrics, and voting on activities. Such initiatives are certainly on the right track as they reflect the teacher's willingness to share decision making with the students. It is, however, only the first step in thinking about what democracy means.

Dewey states, "A democracy is more than a form of government; it is primarily a mode of associated living, of conjoint communicated experience."[4] If so, then the emphasis on social relationships and the well-being of the society plays a critical role in discussions about democracy. It implies that we are not just concerned with political governance but also the ways in which people live together in a good, just society.

Thus, how students work and play together has significance in understanding the multiple dimensions of democracy. Teachers, for instance, might demonstrate democratic practice when they build communities of learning and nurture individuals to reach their full potential. The key idea here is "social." Democracy is about people who must find fair and reasonable ways to live with one another. This could not be more applicable to the school/classroom where students spend a large majority of their day as part of a community.

Democracy also gives rise to the human spirit. Our relationships, in a democratic society, depend on mutual regard for one another. We have the space to be expressive and the means to publicly recognize contributions to our society. At its best, democracy provides freedom to nurture the self.[5] Thus democracy has at least three critical dimensions—"of government, community and the human spirit."[6]

The educational ramification for this multi-dimensional construct is this: if we believe in the "rightness" of a democratic society, then schools must be nothing less than microcosms of this society. In response, those calling for the schools as living examples of democratic practice permeate the educational literature.[7] Democracy and education share so many fundamental ideas that they are "inextricably connected and should be thought of as parts of the same vision."[8]

This brings us to the mission of schooling. What is the purpose of schooling in our American society? According to Goodlad, "the mission of schooling comes down to two related kinds of enculturation; no other institution is so charged. The first is for political and social responsibility as a citizen. The second is for maximum individual development, for full participation in the human conversation."[9]

Michelli offers a similar perspective. He lists the four purposes as: (a) preparing students for critical democratic participation, (b) providing access to knowledge and fostering critical thinking, (c) helping students have full access to life's choices, and (d) preparing students to lead rich and rewarding personal lives.[10]

It is important to note that not all people agree with these purposes. For some, the purpose of education is job preparation and enhancement of the economy. Current-day politicians might argue that the purpose of education is to acquire knowledge that can be measured by tests. I would submit that

Goodlad and Michelli offer a broader vision of schooling that speaks not only to the responsibility of an active participant in a democracy but also to the skills and ways of knowing that lead to a good life.

If one accepts this vision of schooling, then, our mission as teachers is to prepare students for life beyond the school walls—students who can think responsibly and critically about issues that affect society. More importantly, schools need to develop citizens who understand the processes involved in bringing about meaningful change. This suggests that public schools have a greater purpose than transmitting knowledge. Schools have an obligation to educate students for a better future society. [11]

Linda Darling-Hammond, longtime advocate for the public schools, affirms the integral role that democracy plays in the school. She believes that schools have a responsibility to provide experiences where students learn to think critically and participate socially in a community built on democratic principles. "To accomplish this, schools must enact democracy rather than merely preach about it." [12]

Despite the moral argument for teaching students about and through democratic practice, many schools have neither the conditions in place nor the joint administrative-faculty support for realizing this mission. Because democracy grows from the bottom up *and* the top down, individual teachers cannot put large-scale changes into place without some administrative support. It is frustrating to form active learning communities in the classroom when administrators evaluate and reward teachers for a tightly controlled, authoritative style of teaching. Even more disturbing is an emphasis on testing that standardizes learning into short measureable units rather than providing opportunities for students to make reasoned judgments about the messy, ambiguous problems that characterize life.

Meier states, "If a foreign enemy sought to undermine our democracy, it would be hard for them to come up with a better design than the schools we have." [13] This rings true especially for urban schools that perpetuate top-down approaches both in administration and in the classroom. Without teaching methodologies that foster creative thinking and problem solving, students grow to passively accept the system as a given rather than one in which they have the agency to change. Having the power to effect change is particularly pressing in large, unwieldy urban settings. And, while urban students may have the greatest need for systemic transformation, they are often the least empowered to do so. [14]

One of the challenges to democratic practice in the urban schools is an upper-level administration that endorses centralization of schooling process. Strict adherence to poorly designed curricula and endless paperwork becomes the operational standard. In such situations, teachers feel as though they spend more time complying with bureaucratic nonsense than teaching their students. As Meier describes, "We [the school faculty] spoke a lot about democracy, but we were also just plain sick and tired of having to waste so much time and energy negotiating with school officials over what seemed like common sense requests, worrying about myriad rules and regulations, being forced to compromise on so many of our beliefs."[15]

When school policies and curricula are largely driven by those furthest away from the classroom, teachers lose more than just decision-making opportunities. They also lose the right to collaborate in decisions that directly affect their classroom duties. No one teaches at his/her best when his/her professional judgment is not taken seriously.

An incident at WGS illuminated just how electric a situation can become when administrators tighten their grip for control over most aspects of the schooling process. As way of explanation, our head teacher suddenly left WGS to take another position in the district. We then had a wonderful opportunity to find someone whose leadership style was more in keeping with the democratic principles we were trying to model. Given the nature of democratic practice, the faculty expected to have a part in the deliberations over various candidates. Despite certain promises, however, no one from our small faculty was invited to take part in the interview process. It wasn't until the closing minutes of the school day that the dean of the partnering university asked us to join the interviews.

> March 10: *As my colleague and I entered the room, the district supervising principal was completely taken by surprise. (Why hadn't he been told we were coming?) In a fluster, he demanded to know why we were there while other district staff murmured "breach of protocol." He continued to rant, "How can these people be part of an interview process?" "This is outrageous." "They have no qualifications for this."*
>
> *In front of the candidate, the supervising principal and the dean argued back and forth about the nature of democratic practice versus the rules and regulations of the district union. Interestingly, the union representative was not opposed to our presence, which only fueled the flames. The whole thing was very embarrassing and I was angry. How dare these small people pontificate about our lack of qualifications or question our capability for participating in the search process? This was our school too.*

For the hundredth time, I was reminded of the tensions that arise when trying to share decision making on substantive issues. While it may be tough to introduce democratic practice in the classroom, it is aggravating to build a democratic school within a system that operates on an entirely different paradigm. If sharing decision making is frightening for the teacher, how much more so it is for those who believe their position entitles them to a louder voice than the others.

Democracy, by its very nature, cannot be forced upon anyone. It requires the mutual assent of individual and group to respect certain conditions that allow democracy to flourish. Soder articulates these conditions in the book, *Developing Democratic Character in the Young*.[16] His list encompasses the essential principles of a healthy democratic society, which I have then translated to conditions required in a democratic school. The following items represent a selected sampling from Soder's writing:

- Trust: In order to move forward, educators, administrators, students, and the community must feel assured that there is mutual regard for each other. Lack of trust creates a distancing effect in which neither group believes that the other has its best interests at heart. Democracy does not progress in a straight line nor is it without turbulence. It is during these times, more so than those of relative stability, that stakeholders need to trust they are all working toward the same goal. Soder reminds us, "The challenge in human affairs is not to have things go perfectly. The challenge is how to maintain equilibrium while things are falling apart."[17]
- Social capital: To function as a community, people need both the social and political skills to work together. This provides a common framework for sensing and solving problems. When teachers, administrators, and parents come together for the purpose of building a democratic school, they bring different perspectives, resources, and strengths. These combined assets lead not only to the richness of the conversation but also acknowledge the unique perspectives that each stakeholder contributes to the process. Thus, a healthy school is one in which all persons connected to the school believe in the special qualities and experiences that each brings to the table.
- Respect for civil discourse: Part of building trusting relationships comes from the ability to talk, negotiate, and argue one's point of view in the safety of a concerned public. In schools we need to believe that civil discourse plays a critical role in effecting change or solving problems, whether with colleagues or with students.
- Recognition of the need for *e pluribus unum*: In a democracy there is always tension between the individual and the group. This is especially important because classrooms or schools can become satellites traveling their own course without a common purpose. Thus, while we celebrate individual diversity, we also recognize that, ultimately, individuality must also serve the common good.
- Free and open inquiry: The freedom to question and debate without fear of reprisal is one of the most valued human rights in a democracy. Principals who welcome feedback and criticism do so because they feel that such

discussion is beneficial to the school at large. Teachers who open the door to diverse and possibly unpopular points of view do so because it provides for a stimulating learning environment.

- Recognition of the tension between freedom and order: This is one of the more difficult conditions of democracy to address in the classroom. While students need the freedom to talk about ideas and ask questions, a sense of order must prevail to keep the classroom a safe and peaceable learning space. Students need boundaries that provide structure, yet also flexibility. Without order, student energy becomes dissipated in vying for the teacher's attention or struggling to gain power among peers. Freedom always takes place in a context. In the classroom context, teachers must maintain a balance between rules that suppress critical or imaginative thought and a laissez-faire environment that evades focus or guidance.

Soder's list provides a powerful starting place for thinking about democratic practice and assessing where we are in the process. Ostensibly, the conditions that underlie democracy in American society are akin to those that provide a democratic foundation in the school. The conditions of democracy, if practiced in the classroom or school, are not just another fad in education but, rather, a sound approach to schooling embedded in the larger American community.

With this in mind, it is easy to see what was missing in the relationship between university and school district (see journal entry for March 10). Trust and respect for civil discourse, among others, were disturbingly absent from that conversation. Moreover, the events that took place suggested that the district had a different view about the role of democracy in the school. This was not a good sign.

A democratic school or classroom can only go so far without support from the top. This is the highly political nature of democratic schooling—those invested in school-based democracy ought to be at the same table. Disagreement and turf conflicts are inevitable. After all, building a democracy involves gains and losses. What one gains in the freedom to participate, one loses in the efficiency of following orders. What one gains in the freedom of decision making, one loses in the power to control outcomes.

At the school level, a principal can do much to support the democratic classroom. The principal who includes faculty and representatives from the community in substantive decisions, or makes common time for teachers to plan instruction together, promotes an attitude of "we're all in this boat together." The principal who asks teachers to present innovative ideas at a faculty meeting or involves teachers in maintaining the democratic mission of the school shows a sense of commitment that supports individual teachers in their effort to democratize the classroom.

In a traditional school, however, the bulk of democratizing the classroom often falls on the teacher's shoulders, either because there is no support from the administration or the faculty is unwilling to engage in substantive discourse about democratic schooling. Even under these circumstances, teachers can still make a difference albeit the process may progress more slowly and encounter more potholes along the road. As Kincheloe remarks:

> A critical urban pedagogy studies the context of education for the purpose of enhancing human agency—the capacity to act in transformative ways—not to minimize it. Such a pedagogy fervently believes that brilliant and committed urban teachers can make a positive difference in the lives of students and communities, no matter how bad the situation may be. [18]

The beginnings of a democratic classroom rest on at least four essential conditions. First, democracy starts with a trusting relationship. Students need to feel that the teacher is not only interested in their well-being but also looking out for their best interests. Is the classroom safe for students to ask questions and pursue interesting ideas? Does the teacher (sometimes with the students) set reasonable boundaries that curb behavior that disturbs the learning of others? Do teachers and students feel free to think outside the box?

Second, democracy rests on the power of decision making. Not all decisions are appropriate for student participation but in many instances the teacher can integrate substantial decision making in daily teaching strategies. Teaching through problem solving or giving various options for approaching a project are two ideas for approaching subject matter.

Classroom assignments can be prepared with two or three different tiers to meet the diverse ability levels of students in the class. For example, after learning the principles of graphing, the math teacher might ask students to choose one of three graphing problems that vary in complexity. Although some high-ability students may choose the easiest problem to solve, it is just as likely that a low-ability student will choose a more complicated graphing problem. The different levels of complexity, however, give students the incentive to work at their own pace while also engaging in the kind of thinking that supports the concept presented.

Third, democratically oriented teachers recognize the human dimension of each adolescent under their care. Sometimes students make hurtful remarks that require intervention on the part of the teacher. Whether teachers choose to ignore the incident, or see it as an opportunity for learning something important about how people relate to one another, says something about the teacher's philosophical grounding in democratic principles.

Fourth, democracy calls for action, not merely talk. [19] Those who help students learn the various channels for changing policy are teaching students to take control of their lives. Teachers are also helping students to find their voice and develop their skills to effect change. Teaching students to act thoughtfully and compassionately within the context of the situation facilitates both maturity and the know-how to negotiate a complicated system.

In the ideal situation both administrators and educators support a common mission toward democratic practice. The administrator establishes a macro-structure in which teachers are supported in their endeavor to democratize the classroom and the teachers promote access to a quality education for all students. According to Beane and Apple:

> Democratic schools, like democracy itself, do not happen by chance. They result from explicit attempts by educators to put in place arrangements and opportunities that will bring democracy to life. These arrangements and opportunities involve two lines of work. One is to create democratic structures and process by which life in the school is carried out. The other is to create a curriculum that will give young people democratic experiences. [20]

It is also informative to see models of excellent schools where students are engaged in learning and the environment buzzes with purposeful activity. Although conferences often spotlight schools of demonstrated excellence, one gets a more meaningful experience when seeing a school in action. A visitation would, of course, require release time—an encouraging indicator that administrators value ideas that lead to growth in one's own school.

In April, a few of my colleagues and I were invited to visit an inner-city high school with a strong record of accomplishment. This high school had not only been the subject of several TV news programs but also evidenced a 99 percent college placement of its students. We were immediately impressed when students greeted us politely and confidently took us on a tour of the school. All the students we met had an air of confidence. They were enthusiastic about showing the school and talking about their experiences. The staff and principal were also very accommodating in talking about their school and answering questions.

Once over the initial "wow" factor, a few things caught my eye. In every classroom the students were seated in traditional rows and columns with the teacher standing at the blackboard. I saw no discussion-oriented instruction, only students answering questions or quietly taking notes. I asked some teachers if they shared in the decision making about curriculum or felt that they had a significant role in setting policies for the school. Although the answer was "no," it did not seem to be not an issue for those with whom we talked. In fact the teachers seemed very happy to come to work. They appeared quite dedicated to the students and their achievement.

I realize that a one-time visit can lead to assumptions that do not characterize the school as a whole. Yet, the visit was illuminating in many respects:

April 26: *As I think about our visit, I cannot help but compare it with our school. What would visitors see if they came to WGS? On one hand, our school has a completely different model when it comes to shared decision making and curriculum. On the other hand, I wonder whether urban children perform much better in the environment that we observed than in the democratic context that we are trying to establish.*

The school had structures in place that urban students need so desperately. Yet, if teachers are marginalized from decisions that effect their classrooms, how much more so are students who sit quietly in rows and columns? As illustrated in Paolo Friere's work, students must learn how to negotiate the web of politics in order to affect changes that impact their lives. Perhaps the other school excelled because rules and regulations had been firmly established. We definitely fall short in this area. I am confused. Everything seems to work so beautifully in that school . . . except for a sense of democratic practice.

Although our school still felt moderately chaotic, some things were improving. The science teacher invited students to plant a garden in the back of the school. Students came on their spring break, voluntarily, and felt a sense of pride when the garden was finished. The language arts teacher and social studies teacher had students engaged in individual or small-group projects. Music class became a creative outlet for students to express their own individuality rather than a constant battle for control.

Despite this progress the question remains: "Is democracy worth it?" Would we trade our chaos for a school in which students were quiet and orderly but taught in a traditional top-down approach? How important is it that students and teachers have a voice in the schooling process when the school down the street yields such spectacular gains in student achievement? But, what is it that they are achieving and how are they achieving it?

It is naïve to approach schooling from an either/or situation—either the school is chaotic in its democratic evolution or the school is rule-bound and progressing efficiently. No doubt the emergence of democracy is not without its bumps and bruises. Building genuine relationships and sharing decision making opens the door to a cacophony of voices, sometimes in heated conversation.

Students have strong opinions. Teachers have a right to voice their thinking about school practice. Administrators have the power to create learning spaces that support a diversity of views. And, yes, this is a noisy, often uncomfortable process.

While our hearts and minds were in the right place at WGS, there were things to be learned from that school down the street. Too much chaos, for instance, diverts energy away from the business of democratic schooling. Too much shared decision making has the potential for stultifying the process. In a democratic school, there need to be structures that sustain order while still creating leaders.

We want to nurture independently minded individuals while also building an environment of shared concern for the common good.[21] We want students to engage in collaborative projects but we also want students to learn something about getting along with other people. In short, there are many things that other schools can teach us without our losing sight of the big picture.

Good schools achieve this balance in different ways; however the outcomes are a telling indicator of what the school values. When schools value the rights of students, teachers, administrators, and community members in building a school together, then we should expect: (a) students who lead through thoughtfulness and compassion, (b) teachers who care about the well-being of students through nurturing behaviors and academically rigorous curriculums, (c) administrators who sustain focus on the democratic mission, and (d) community members who have a voice in the schooling enterprise.

A school district, school, or classroom that reflects democratic practice at its best also contributes to the common good of society. Democracy, as with education, is a liberating process. The two work hand in hand, not as separate entities but as cojoined partners. Levin writes, "In this extended view, democracy still involves individuals and their participation in decisions, but places them within a larger and fuller concept of a community life and a set of cultural practices."[22]

To work well, a democracy must be self-sustaining. One cannot expect people to participate openly and actively in a democracy without having had such experiences in the past. Darling-Hammond comments, "So much is democracy an American birthright, so deeply do Americans believe that we embody and define democracy that we often take its existence and its practice for granted in our own nation."[23]

We can do more in our public schools to assure the sustenance of our American democracy. If we want to live in a healthy democracy with all of its rights and privileges, then schools must provide spaces for exercising democratic thought and action. According to Beane and Apple, "Many people believe that democracy is nothing more than a form of federal government and thus does not apply to schools and other social institutions. Many also believe that democracy is a right of adults, not of young people. And some believe that democracy simply cannot work in schools."[24] Can we put up with the tussles of associative living and the long, difficult process of effecting social change? I submit that we can, if we feel it is worth it.

NOTES

1. Roger Soder, "Education for Democracy: The Foundation for Democratic Character," in *Developing Democratic Character in the Young,* ed. Roger Soder, John I. Goodlad, and Timothy J. McMannon (San Francisco: Jossey-Bass, 2001), 186.

2. Roger Soder, "Democracy—Do We Really Want It?" in *The Public Purposes of Education and Schooling,* ed. John I. Goodlad and Timothy J. McMannon (San Francisco: Jossey-Bass, 1997), 85.

3. James A. Beane and Michael W. Apple, "The Case for Democratic Schools," in *Democratic Schools,* ed. Michael W. Apple and James A. Beane (Alexandria, VA: Association for Supervision and Curriculum Development, 1995), 22.

4. John Dewey, *Democracy and Education* (Middlesex, England: Echo Library, 2007), 68.

5. Donna H. Kerr, "Toward a Democratic Rhetoric of Schooling," in *The Public Purposes of Education and Schooling,* ed. John I. Goodlad and Timothy J. McMannon (San Francisco: Jossey-Bass, 1997), 73–84.

6. John I. Goodlad, "Democracy, Education, and Community," in *Democracy, Education, and the Schools,* ed. Roger Soder (San Francisco: Jossey-Bass, 1997), 100.

7. See, for example, Apple and Beane, *Democratic Schools*; John I. Goodlad, *Educational Renewal: Better Teachers, Better Schools* (San Francisco: Jossey-Bass, 1994).

8. Benjamin Levin, "The Educational Requirement for Democracy," *Cultural Inquiry* 28 (1998): 63.

9. Goodlad, "Democracy, Education, and Community," 112.

10. Nicholas M. Michelli, "Education in a Democracy: Why, How and What?: Examining the Current State of Policy and Practice, and Relating to the Role of Education in a Democracy in the United States," Centre for Governance and Citizenship Working Paper Series No. 2011/001 (The Hong Kong Institute of Education, January 2011), 4–10. http://www.ied.edu.hk/cgc/view.php?secid=900.

11. Dewey, *Democracy and Education*.

12. Linda Darling-Hammond, "Education, Equity, and the Right to Learn," in *The Public Purposes of Education and Schooling,* ed. John I. Goodlad and Timothy J. McMannon (San Francisco: Jossey-Bass, 1997), 47.

13. Deborah W. Meier, "Undermining Democracy: 'Compassionate Conservatism' and Democratic Education," *Dissent* 53, no. 4 (2006): 72.

14. See, for example, Darling-Hammond, "Education, Equity, and the Right to Learn"; Dennis Shirley, "Promoting Participatory Democracy through Community Organizing," in *Partnering to Prepare Urban Teachers: A Call to Activism,* ed. Francine P. Peterman (New York: Peter Lang, 2008), 59–76.

15. Deborah Meier, *The Power of Their Ideas: Lessons for America from a Small School in Harlem* (Boston: Beacon, 1995), 23.

16. Soder, "Education for Democracy," 189–192.

17. Soder, "Education for Democracy," 188.

18. Joe Kincheloe, "Why a Book on Urban Education?" in *19 Urban Questions: Teaching in the City,* ed. Shirley R. Steinberg and Joe L. Kincheloe, (New York: Peter Lang, 2007), 17.

19. Soder, "Education for Democracy."

20. Beane and Apple, "The Case for Democratic Schools," 9.

21. William Ayers, "Teaching In and For Democracy," *Curriculum and Teaching Dialogue* 12, no. 1/2 (2009–2010), 3–10.

22. Levin, "Educational Requirement," 61.

23. Linda Darling-Hammond, "Democracy and Access to Education," in *Democracy, Education, and the Schools,* ed. Roger Soder (San Francisco: Jossey-Bass, 1996), 151.

24. Beane and Apple, "The Case for Democratic Schools," 7.

Chapter Eleven

The Arts as Democratic Practice

There is no more powerful agent in communicating the ideals of democracy than through the arts. How we define art, however, is controversial and contemporary philosophers have written many treatises on this very subject. For the purposes of this chapter I am broadly defining the arts as activity within the visual arts, music, dance, theater, and literature. In addition, I see the arts as inclusive of both Western and non-Western genres. While this definition is simplistic and not traditionally accepted by all, it serves as a starting point for this chapter.

In terms of democracy, art is a beacon of free speech and a canvas for imagination and creative insight. The arts nurture not only problem solving but also diverse ways of thinking that transcend political borders. And, although the role of the arts in democracy is often overshadowed by an ever-present hum of political conversation, the arts remain essential to the democratic fabric of our society. Consequently, "No consideration of the relationship between education and democracy is complete without examining the importance of the arts in a democratic society."[1]

Conversations about the arts are particularly relevant in education for both arts specialists and "non-arts" teachers. When not besieged by budget cuts and reduction of qualified faculty, schools have an opportunity to link issues of democracy with artworks. In essence, the content of art can have as much learning import as the technique and craftsmanship used in creating the work.

While discipline, passion, and creativity are often cited as outcomes of artistic activity, the arts also provides numerous opportunities for exploring social issues and themes of social justice. On one hand, the *teaching* of art is, in itself, an issue of social justice. We must be mindful of who receives a quality level of arts instruction and who does not. On the other hand, we can use artwork as a catalyst for discussing issues of social justice. Often these issues illuminate how we construct meaning from art.

For example, "On the Transmigration of Souls," a Pulitzer Prize–winning composition by John Adams, was written to commemorate the traumatic events of 9/11. The piece superimposes prerecorded street sounds and the reading of victim's names on a stunning symphonic palette of orchestral music. Although one need not have special training to appreciate Adams's work, a teacher can help students move beyond images of smoldering wreckage to a profound lesson on the agony of loss and the celebration of life. A good music teacher can expand this experience to explore the musical devices that Adams used to create these images and expression through sound.

At WGS, the musical *West Side Story* began as a lesson based on questions of social justice but soon blossomed into a full-scale creative arts project. Because students were reading *Romeo and Juliet*, the musical served as a natural bridge from Shakespeare to a more contemporary setting. Although the libretto was somewhat dated in terms of language, students could easily relate to the themes of gang activity, racial tension, and adolescent love. According to Carter, "The teaching of aesthetics in urban education is better understood if tied to lived experiences within the urban environment—its people, languages, homes, neighborhoods, families, authorities, actions, and exchange that take place between these and other facets that illustrate experience as the reflection of understanding for the urban student."[2]

While the parallels between *West Side Story* and *Romeo and Juliet* are not unique, the idea came at just the right time. Spring had moved quickly into summer temperatures and the students were hot, angry, and sick of school. They needed a creative project that involved group work and independent thinking. For that reason, the students and I decided that each of the four classes would write and direct an original play based on themes from the musical.

April 29: *There is a lot of excitement surrounding this project. The students come in ready to work with absolutely no patience for anyone who fools around. They are extremely serious about their part in making the play come together. I think that the following factors play a large role in the productive behavior that I see: (a) students developed their own characters and created the story; (b) students chose the activities that they wanted to participate in (e.g., artist, actor); (c) the classes are highly organized: each activity has an assessment folder and team leader, and there are plenty of things to do even for students who are not yet involved with the "heavy" stuff; and (d) the activities represent a broad range of interests . . . from dance to computer work. These students crave "hands-on" learning. They want to perform, they want to be out there, and they like making art. They need this expressive outlet.*

Guiding students through a large-scale creating project is not without its obstacles. Often one group needed finished work from another group in order to proceed. This created lag time for some students while others worked. Other times the space felt too small to support actors in one corner, dancers in another and everyone else in between. To push forward with such a project, teachers must not only embrace the concept of "works in progress" but also the discomfort of minor confusion as students struggle with challenging problems.

Snyder states, "The arts are about empowering learners, and the social/emotional advantages of arts-infused learning are paramount to success in school and life. For disenfranchised students and teachers, this approach affords a new opportunity for success."[3] When students stumble through their academic classes, the arts can offer a different medium for personal expression and high-level cognitive activity. "As a tool of critical inquiry," Carter writes, "the arts can provide a nontraditional framework for teaching concepts of beauty and value to the urban student."[4] Moreover, the arts also give a platform to students whose voices are not always heard or taken seriously.

A teacher who is sensitive to the dual role of democracy and art creates an environment for students to think creatively, critically, and thoughtfully. Such dispositions are central not only to democratic practice but also in examining or making works of art. For this reason, it is important to recognize that art is a teacher in all disciplines and not the sole purview of the art specialist. Although the art specialist lends particular expertise in examining works of art, any teacher can use art to help students interpret and respond to the world around them.

As a prompt for a creative writing assignment, for instance, consider Van Gogh's *Starry Night*, with its swirling night sky punctuated by luminous orbs and orange crescent moon. Notice the contrast of the expansive sky with the tiny village below. Whatever captivates our imagination, this painting means something, partly because many of us have experienced the miracle of a starry night, but mostly because we have the opportunity to view this night sky through someone else's soul.

Knowing something about Van Gogh's deeply troubled soul, and the fact that he painted *Starry Night* in 1889 nearing the end of his voluntary stay in the asylum at Saint Rémy-de-Provence lends particular poignancy to the painting. This additional layer of understanding brings new meaning to the way one perceives the work. It also speaks to the contextual variables that influence how we experience art.

A good teacher can bring all of these aspects together, including a discussion of how artists contribute to society in spite of difficult life challenges. Urban youth themselves are no strangers to adversity. For some students, conversations about *Starry Night* could become the gateway for discovering art as a medium for responding to hardship.

In our American society, we have not done enough to cultivate thoughtful consumers of art. Arts programs are among the first to be cut out of the public school budget. Administrators find clever ways to save money by maintaining the art program but cutting the budget for materials. Equally egregious is the practice of combining classes so that arts classes can reach nearly sixty students or beyond.

According to Ross, "Schools' priorities do not enable—but rather, they disable—students, particularly those from minority or new immigrant populations from becoming imaginative through artistic literacy."[5] While Ross admits that "art costs money," he also says that "the perennial problem is not really about money; it is the public's very dim perception of what the arts do for society and for people as individuals."[6] This distressing statement leads us back to the schools and the powerful role that schools can, yet often do not, play in arts education.

In the urban schools, the situation for arts education is not a positive one. Although urban schools are often the recipient of large arts grants, these programs survive as long as the funding holds out and then disappear. What urban schools lack, in terms of the arts, is continuity. Haphazardly moving arts teachers among buildings or levels of schooling (e.g., elementary, middle school) has damaging consequences for arts programs, which take years to cultivate. Hiring arts teachers as prep time providers rather than artist educators speaks volumes about the school's willingness to invest in quality arts programs. For non-artist teachers, then, the demand to include arts increases. However many teachers do not know how to integrate arts into the general subject areas.

Non-arts teachers often feel intimidated about using art in the classroom, where, in fact, art could have a powerful impact on the learning process. Some believe it is the art specialist's job to educate students in the arts. Others think they need special talent to teach with art—"I can't even sing a tune." This suggests that somewhere along the line, teachers have not had the kinds of positive art experiences that inspire them to continue these experiences with their students. For youth, meaningful encounters with the arts can take place in any subject if guided by a skillful teacher. Teacher education programs can do considerably more to advance arts literacy among those who choose a career in education. Perhaps we spend too much time using text and talk as the medium of instruction, forgetting to include art as a mode of inquiry. In thinking about teacher education some questions arise: "What if we truly believe that art is a distinct, essential intelligence[7] and that to strengthen our programs through the arts is to strengthen the larger community?" "Would teacher education recognize that developing art-sensitive teachers is critical to a full and comprehensive education?" "How would this change the way we go about educating the teachers who will then educate the students?"

Ideally, methods classes in the sciences and humanities would integrate art into teaching strategies with the understanding that art is a unique form of communication that illuminates content from a different perspective. For example, elementary teachers often use songs to help students remember lists or facts, for example, the "alphabet song." While this is a good way to remember the order of the letters, it is not an arts lesson. An arts-infused lesson uses art as a form of critical inquiry. In an arts-focused curriculum, a social studies lesson about the Civil War might include authentic songs from the era to illustrate music as a means of showing patriotism, keeping troops in step, or expressing longing for loved ones left behind.

For pre-service teachers in the arts, lessons would invite students to explore the social context as means of deepening students' artistic experiences. "Even today," Woodford remarks, "music teacher 'training' still emphasizes traditional pedagogical knowledge over social or other forms of inquiry, while academics have yet to adequately conceptualize music education's role or function in democratic society."[8] When works of art do not lend themselves to specific issues of social justice, discussions or tasks that facilitate critical thinking continue to develop habits of mind essential in an evolving democracy.

None of these ideas calls for radical changes in teacher education, but rather they seek to demystify the arts as a teaching tool for artists only. Art brings a unique dimension to learning that no other discipline can emulate. It also reflects the spirit of democracy, in design or as a creative act. Darling-Hammond states, "Democratic life requires access to forms of knowledge that enable creative life and thought as well as access to a social dialogue that enables democratic communication and participation."[9] Consequently, the creative thought and life of a child is too precious to overlook.

June 15: *Last night my students performed their original plays at an end-of-the-year celebration for faculty and families. From an educational perspective, I couldn't have hoped for more. The students showed tremendous growth in their acting and staging skills. I saw shy, inhibited students flourish in front of an audience. I saw students who never set foot on stage and who may never have the opportunity again, revel in the applause and laughter of an apprecia- tive audience. And, I saw a few students filled with possibilities of further theatrical work given this small chance to perform in a school production.*
The performances, however, had some major flaws. It was hard to hear a lot of the students because they had no microphone. This made it difficult to follow the plot. In their nervousness, students missed their cues or paced the action so quickly that it was difficult to interpret. Later that night, in the quiet of my home, I pondered whether student pride and individual accomplishment was good enough. If the democratic process contributed to the students' confidence and competence yet results in a substandard product, have I, in reality, failed my students?

In creative work, where a spirit of democracy is essential to artistic freedom, there is no promise that the artwork will ultimately satisfy the artist or the public. When artists begin to compose or draw, they do so with a conception in mind but no guarantee of a successful outcome. History is replete with stories of failed premieres and miserable reviews (although many of those art pieces survived to become icons of the discipline). The arts in education, however, have a different purpose.

In education the goal is not so much to create great works of art as it is to help students become more refined and sophisticated in their artistic decision making. When an art product is not involved, the goal is to experience art with heightened sensitivity to its context and its properties. Thus, teaching art through a democratic lens has meaning when it creates more thoughtful, feelingful human beings. In other words, teachers must sometimes sacrifice artistry for the sake of a larger educational goal.

While this may sound oversimplified, it is often the root of difficult dilemmas in day-to-day teaching. For instance, who should a teacher choose for an important role in the play: a weak but hard-working, enthusiastic student or a less reliable, more talented student who will, if he/she shows up, delight and engage the audience? Comparably, what if an outgoing, personable child chooses to design a program cover instead of seeking an acting role, which would contribute much more to the success of the performance?

These dilemmas were inherent in the decision to have WGS students create their own plays. Encouraged to work in their areas of interest (e.g., playwright, actor, dancer, art design), students often made unpredictable choices. Sometimes their choice reflected an interest but not a particular strength. Had I directed the play and assigned students to various roles, the play might have had a more polished performance. Yet, allowing the students to decide their own roles not only strengthened their personal investment in the project but also opened the door for those who wanted to learn something new.

It is a hard decision to publicly display student work that does not meet a certain standard but does, in fact, have meaning to the child involved. Exhibiting a student's immature pencil drawing or including a Down syndrome child in a dance recital who has less motor coordination than other dancers—these are dilemmas that accompany a democratic approach. I am not advocating that teachers disregard the quality of the student's work, but rather, suggesting that sometimes students make greater and more lasting gains when they have a substantive part in the process.

The arts, and for that matter, teaching in general, will always involve public criticism and scrutiny. From the standpoint of the teacher, it is important to understand that every decision is made within a context. There are times when we choose the less able child for an important role because the gains for that child outweigh the needs of the group. Conversely, teachers with a democratic agenda often face the reality that the decisions they make, while in the best interest of the student, may be misunderstood or judged unfairly by the spectator.

To many, the arts and democracy seem like separate conversations. Some art critics would even argue that democracy has no place in an arts curriculum. Concurrently, many teachers would place the study of democracy exclusively within the social studies or history curriculum. Yet art and democracy share similar fundamental attributes. Both are anchored in a social context that encourages creating and reflection. Both honor disparate points of view, whether in agreement or not. And, both celebrate the freedom to express ideas in the spirit of humanity.

There are numerous implications for teaching. On one hand, arts education serves a valuable function by helping even the youngest students experience works of art and some level of discourse about art. The arts help us come to know our place in history and culture. This suggests that the arts are not the sole responsibility of the arts specialists, but, rather, that art literacy crosses disciplinary lines. Interdisciplinary study, when coordinated by teachers of like minds and goals, can become some of the most powerful learning experiences for students. This type of teaching lends itself to all students but particularly those students whose lives are already splintered in terms of stability, emotional closeness, and artistic sensitivity.

On the other hand, teachers who teach from mechanized scripts or engage students in token arts experiences (e.g., watching a PowerPoint presentation that includes accompanying music) do little to forward the place of arts in a comprehensive curriculum. Woodford states, "The last thing music teachers should want is to remain slaves to overly prescriptive pedagogies and methodologies that may well stifle the thinking and creativity of their students."[10] Further, "If democracy is the end, then the democratic rights and responsibilities of all concerned ought to be constantly in view in classes, lessons, or rehearsals, as should any democratic principles."[11]

Sometimes arts specialists approach urban students with the mistaken notion that they know nothing about art, given their limited experience with the fine arts. They often begin with the classics without recognizing that urban areas are teeming with arts. Students live in a world of hip-hop and graffiti. They can easily discern style and critique performance in familiar genres. According to Carter,

> The urban stage has already provided the student with tools to build a critique of aesthetic quality. This view must be recognized and respected. The urban student is expected to adapt to the aesthetic standards as historically defined by the institution of school. But does the school look to adapt and learn the new aesthetic qualities and values embodied by the urban student?[12]

Here is a wonderful starting place for democratic practice to begin. The urban adolescent's world is rife with issues of social justice, communicated through rap, slam poetry, and bold expressions through drawings. These forms of art are accessible to all teachers and provide the impetus for examining issues that affect these students' lives. Starting with art of the city, then, becomes a bridge for exploring less familiar art forms in both Western and non-Western genres. Ross acknowledges, "The simple truth is that there must be a vital connection between art, artists, and education in the arts and a conscious realization by the public that the arts make for the public good."[13] For this reason, teachers who teach for democratic practice realize that understanding the social framework of the artwork often leads to a deeper artistic experience.

Urban students, as creative and responsive to the arts as any other students, desperately need the arts in their schooling. Because they are particularly disadvantaged when it comes to extracurricular arts experiences, the schools must consider three requisite conditions to teaching democracy through the arts. First, arts teachers must recognize the essential role that arts play in the lives of their students, both as a means of personal expression and a means of developing intellectually mature citizens. Second, all teachers should view art as a gateway to discussing issues of social justice, and third, administrators must preserve the integrity of the arts by supporting arts-infused instruction and collaboration between the non-arts teacher and the arts specialist.

Simply having arts programs in the school, however, does not necessarily mean that quality arts instruction or democratic practice is taking place. "Doing art" does not always signify growth in thoughtfulness about the ways of the world. Woodford, for instance, distinguishes between "music as a drug to which mere exposure or immersion is supposed to make children happier and more civilized (albeit rendered passive) and music and music classes as occasions for the development of musical, intellectual, and moral character."[14]

Working with the arts as democratic practice is, in effect, good teaching. It relies on student-centered instruction, critical thinking, and contextualized problem solving. The key to successful integration of art and democracy lies in the teacher's skill to raise questions of social justice without sacrificing content knowledge or its particular parameters.

A good teacher recognizes that substantive experiences with art are different from exposure to art. Whereas exposure to art provides a cursory experience with an art object, substantive art experiences involve attending to the properties (e.g., use of rhythmic qualities) of an artwork as well as finding connections between art and its social context. Democratic practice calls for arts professionals who not only understand their discipline well but also intuitively see connections between the arts and social justice. For arts specialists this means that the goal is not always exclusively focused on the art object, but rather developing students who integrate artistic forms of knowledge as a path toward productive citizenship. This is both teaching art through democracy and teaching democracy through the arts.

Access to the arts is a right of all children, especially for those who are marginalized. In our democratic society we hold dear the freedom of speech. Art, above all, reflects a medium where that freedom can take place regardless of race, creed, religion, gender, or language. Just as we promote access to tangible resources, "democratic life also requires access to empowering forms of knowledge that enable creative life and thought."[15]

The summer camp, Interlochen Center for the Arts in Interlochen, Michigan, has a slogan that reflects the essence of art in society: "Art Lives Here." As such, art *is* the people, their culture, and the world around us. When teachers encourage students to comprehend the purpose of art, its character, and its social context coupled with its formal properties, art can have a profound effect. For urban students, especially, art should open doors rather than become "sites of exclusion and alienation."[16] Surely our students deserve nothing less.

NOTES

1. Nicholas M. Michelli, "Education for Democracy: What Can It Be?" in *Teacher Education for Democracy and Social Justice,* ed. Nicholas M. Michelli and David Lee Keiser (New York: Routledge, 2005), 6.

2. Roymieco A. Carter, "Can Aesthetics Be Taught in Urban Education?" in *19 Urban Questions: Teaching in the City,* ed. Shirley R. Steinberg and Joe L. Kincheloe (New York: Peter Lang, 2007), 243.

3. Susan Snyder, "Arts for All Sakes: Arts-Infused Curriculum as a School Reform Model," in *Teaching Music in the Urban Classroom: A Guide to Leadership, Teacher Education, and Reform,* ed. Carol Frierson-Campbell, vol. 2 (Lanham, MD: Rowman and Littlefield, 2006), 197.

4. Carter, "Can Aesthetics Be Taught?" 231.

5. Jerrold Ross, "Art Education and the Newer Public Good," *Arts Education Policy Review* 106, no. 3 (2005): 6.

6. Ross, "Art Education," 4.

7. Howard Gardner, *Frames of Mind: The Theory of Multiple Intelligences* (New York: Basic Books, 1983).

8. Paul G. Woodford, *Democracy and Music Education: Liberalism, Ethics, and the Politics of Practice* (Bloomington: Indiana University Press, 2005), 13.

9. Linda Darling-Hammond, "Education, Equity, and the Right To Learn," in *The Public Purpose of Education and Schooling,* ed. John I. Goodlad and Timothy J. McMannon (San Francisco: Jossey-Bass, 1997), 44.

10. Woodford, *Democracy and Music Education,* 30.

11. Woodford, *Democracy and Music Education,* 84.

12. Carter, "Can Aesthetics Be Taught?" 231.

13. Ross, "Art Education," 4.

14. Woodford, *Democracy and Music Education,* 85.

15. Linda Darling-Hammond, "Democracy and Access to Education," in *Democracy, Education, and the Schools,* ed. Roger Soder (San Francisco: Jossey Bass, 1996), 161.

16. Carter, "Can Aesthetics Be Taught?" 235.

Chapter Twelve

Lessons Learned

The school year (and my sabbatical) is almost over. I have experienced a world of teaching beyond my wildest imagination and come to know a special group of adolescents that could make your heart sing or your blood pressure rise. It is the sheer range of these experiences and the opportunity to see beyond the students' outward selves from which I have culled the greatest lessons. For it was only through "living" with students that I began to detect the subtext of their behavior and the patterns of human dynamics that lie beneath the surface of ordinary interactions at school.

I came to WGS with the hope of bringing democratic practice into the classroom. I left with the realization that democracy is far more complicated than giving students choices or facilitating discussions to which all have access. My conception of school-based democracy has been tested not only by the students but also by the very structure of the school itself. I now know how hard it is to build a democratic classroom/school when students are hungry or angry or hurt. I know how hard it is to build a democratic classroom/school when all players are not on the same page. Yet, I am more convinced than ever that the process is worth the struggle.

All along, this book has followed the birthing of a democratic school and called attention to the qualities that lead to good teachers as well as good schools. I believe, though, when one introduces the concept of democracy into the equation it raises a compelling question: "What is the difference between a good school and a good school based on a democratic mission?" That teachers should share decision making with students or demonstrate a deep level of caring or engage students in meaningful problem solving—these could be characteristics of any good school. And, even further, is good teaching synonymous with democratic practice?

The difference, I submit, has everything to the reasons for *why* we do what we do. In a school based on democratic principles, the intent of good teaching is not that it produces better test scores or supports the national champion debate team, but that it leads to the development of thoughtful participants in a democratic society.

When we introduce tasks that involve substantive problem solving, we do so with the intent of helping our students recognize that life has many messy problems without clear-cut solutions—"that participants in a democracy are actively skeptical and do not take things for granted."[1] When we teach students to care and to empathize, we do so because a good society depends on associative living and people who think of others while also meeting their needs. When we teach students about apartheid or the Japanese internment camps during World War II, we use these events as the impetus for building leaders who seek justice in an unjust society.

If we believe that the schools are places for building a culture of students who not only participate in a democracy but know the avenues for taking action, then everything we do has a purpose in empowering students to live and lead by democratic principles toward a rich, fulfilling life. Thus, when the school embraces this mission and faculty work toward common goals, a democratically based school *is* a good school.

The urban setting brings unique challenges to school democracy, as students bring a decidedly different perspective of what a school looks like. They often experience the least able teachers who teach via prescriptive methods and see themselves as transmitters of knowledge rather than agents of transformation. Students come to expect mindless worksheets, authoritarian style of teaching, and strict rules for compliance. Student-centered instruction and taking ownership of one's learning may be interpreted as signs of weakness—that the teacher does not know what to teach. A sharing of responsibility for the class and teachers who do not insist on controlling every aspect of the classroom can lead an urban student to believe that the teacher does not know how to teach. Such expectations not only upset a student's feeling for order and stability but also open the door to less than civil behavior.

At WGS, uncivil behavior continued to impede the teaching process. In hindsight, I see that we dove so quickly into a way of teaching inimical to students' expectations that we left them confused and bewildered. Likewise, their behavior left us confused and bewildered. Had we understood the reasons behind the madness, we might have used September as a time to focus on community-building activities and the development of mutual regard for each other. In a school where these habits are already in place, teachers can use content and incidents at school to raise issues about social justice. Our students simply were not ready for this kind of culture when school began.

First and foremost, a democratic school must value relationships and the hard work that goes into maintaining productive relationships. Ayers writes, "Respect for persons, for teachers, and for students, for parents, and community members, is at the core of good democratic schools."[2] Someone walking into a democratic classroom ought to see a number of things in place: (a) mutual respect for students and faculty, (b) an appreciation for a diversity of perspectives, (c) students who listen to other student's ideas, (d) students who question the status quo and give reasoned responses for their position, and (e) a learning environment that has a feeling of peace rather than violence or unfettered anger.[3]

Tightly interfaced with these dispositions is a deep sense of caring for the well-being of the student, both in his/her academic studies and his/her emotional health. All students need caring teachers and for many urban students, school is the one place where students can rely on consistent, unconditional care. Care is as present in demanding high standards as it is in empathic listening to students' own stories. I do believe that students at WGS felt a sense of care in terms of their emotional well-being. In many ways, however, we fell short, not for lack of care, but unknowingly enabling dependency both academically and in personal interactions:

> June 2: *At lunchtime, some students begin to approach teachers for lunch money, despite the fact that they can get special compensation for lunch. Those of us, who rightly or wrongly think the students may starve without our intervention, easily hand over $1.35 or more. I have found that when I do this, students sometimes look at the money as if I have short-changed them. "Is this all?" they ask, and stupidly I feel embarrassed, looking for more change.*

Sure, we cared that students ate a good lunch. Sure, we knew that lunch might be their most nutritional meal of the day and that full stomachs help students focus on challenging work. But, wouldn't it have made more sense to investigate how the school could help the student rather than quietly slipping some change into the student's palm? From a democratic perspective, the school has a moral obligation to ensure that all students have access to equitable resources, including a hot lunch.

Another dimension of care is culturally responsive teaching. In a democratic school, teachers know the community where their students live and they forge professional relationships with the families of their students. Teachers for democratic practice recognize that knowing the family gives insight into how students connect with the world. All of this information translates to instruction that takes the student's culture into account. For example, one of my graduate students begins and ends his classroom newsletters with a Korean salutation. It is a simple gesture but one that the parents of this Korean-dominated school genuinely appreciate because language plays such a critical role in their children's culture.

In addition to family culture, democratically oriented teachers must also respond to the culture of adolescence, the culture of poverty, the cultures of racial diversity, disability, sexual orientation, and so on. To teach with these cultures in mind indicates that teachers care about where students come from, knowing that schooling needs to build many kinds of bridges for learning to take place.

Often teachers see families not as collaborators in education but as the scapegoats for student misbehavior. Unfortunately, we overlook the many parents who care about education and dwell on those who don't come to school events, who keep their child home to babysit, or who seem to abandon their parental responsibilities.

> June 3: *Today, I had lunch with a colleague at a local pizza shop. One of our students and her mother came in to order lunch. While we continued our conversation, the mother was exasperatedly searching her purse for a missing pizza coupon. She was understandably upset and frustrated that she might have to go back to her home to retrieve the coupon. She began hissing, "Shit," "Shit, I can't believe this." Finally, she stood up as if no one else was in the pizza joint and said loudly, "SHIT, I can't find it." Ironically, no one else in the restaurant seemed to notice.*

When such incidents fit into our already distorted picture of urban families, it takes little to generalize such behavior to all caregivers. What started as a public display of questionable behavior quickly morphed into "See, no wonder our students act the way they do. With caregivers like this, how will they learn composure and respect for others around them?"

How naïve it is to look at the small subset of parents who exhibit unconventional behavior in public places and assume that all caregivers act the same way. It is equally unfair to generalize that parents don't care about their students or their students' education. Given the stress of everyday school incidents we tend to forget that many parents have sacrificed dearly, by emigrating to the United States or working several jobs so that their children have an opportunity to better themselves through an education.

A democratic school is a partnership among the students, the faculty and administration, and the community. According to Duncan-Andrade and Morrell, "To be effective, urban education reform movements must begin to develop partnerships with communities that provide young people the opportunity to be successful while maintaining their identities as urban youth."[4] At WGS, we began to form parent committees. This was a step in the right direction but perhaps started a little too late in the school year.

One of the most difficult areas in creating a democratic climate involved persuading the students that they could indeed flourish in an environment that allowed them to think for themselves and take on leadership roles in the classroom. At the beginning of the school year, students responded more readily to the faculty coordinator who yelled a lot and generated strict rules. Because she rarely followed up on these rules and because most of the faculty seemed so gentle by comparison, the students took advantage of what they saw as a school without structure. Thus, throughout the year, I noticed that students fell roughly into three categories:

- The students who were loud, disrespectful, and brazen about getting what they wanted. They consistently called attention to themselves with outrageous behavior that resulted in a discrepancy between the students' code of behavior and the contrasting norms of acceptable school behavior. These students thought nothing of walking into an ongoing class to look for a book, or opening the door and yelling a question to someone in the class. It seemed that the primary purpose of school, for these students, was that of a social meeting house where teachers became the roadblocks toward that end.
- Other students were quiet, serious about school, and hard working. These students seemed to cluster with others like themselves and stayed fairly isolated within their own social group. Despite the fact that these students displayed the qualities most coveted by schools, they had the least opportunity to shine in the classroom. Given the loud, impulsive nature of the more socially oriented students, the high-achieving students not only had less opportunities to speak but also less time to really explain their thinking.
- Some students just gave up on school and it took enormous effort on the part of the teacher to get any kind of activity at all. These students put their heads down during class, refused to participate in groups, and did not engage in any kind of class work. These students neither demanded attention nor got in the way of other students.

Over the year it became painfully obvious that the most disruptive students operated from codes of behavior deemed necessary to survive in the street yet were antithetical to codes of behavior necessary to participate in a democratic climate. Although I found much of the behavior appalling, the offending students felt that my insistence on civility, at times, was equally shocking.

In trying to help students process their behavior or lapses of judgment we encountered strong resistance to accountability. I saw and experienced students who screamed outrage at the teacher for citing some misconduct that they claimed they never committed. Such students were highly defensive and had learned that vehement resistance to blame became a realized perception that, indeed, they had been victimized once again by the schooling enterprise.

Closely related to the resistance of accountability was a feeling of entitle-
ment to anything and everything in the school, from sitting at the secretary's
desk with feet propped up to walking into the teacher's room unannounced
and taking a bottle of water. Few of my students showed any sense of boundaries between private and public spaces. When the faculty asked students
not to come into the faculty room, students reacted with body language that
shouted, "Who do you think you are?"

Although I came to care deeply for my students, and, in the end, tried to
find ways of staying at WGS for a second year, I cannot gloss over the fact
that adolescents, particularly urban adolescents, can be extremely difficult.
To sugarcoat this aspect of teaching, would, in fact, misrepresent the conditions of teaching that we encountered, as do many other urban teachers. It is
complex to deal with human beings, especially adolescents. For not only are
we dealing with the roller-coaster emotions of adolescents, but we are also
dealing with the culture of poverty, the difficulties of immigrants assimilating into American culture, family hardship, and students' coming of age.

Nevertheless, the challenges of working with our students made their
success all the more thrilling. According to Stotko and colleagues, "Effective
urban teachers believe that it is not easy to improve student learning and
performance. They are persistent: they refuse to give up on their students."[5]

I will never forget that sense of pride that my students showed as they
bowed after their first piano recital. I will always remember the passion with
which my students discussed the role of art in society and where their dance
exhibition fit into that role. Most affecting were the small things from day to
day: "Dr. D., music is our favorite class"; "Dr. D., come over and see what
we've composed"; "Dr. D., Beethoven had a really hard life but he made
good music."

I think that when teachers talk about the rewards of teaching urban children, they are not discounting the difficult days but feel so invigorated when
a student finally "gets it." This is a happy moment for all teachers, but for
urban teachers the successes are measured in leaps rather than steps. Kozol's
findings, while oriented toward elementary schools, is relevant to any urban
school:

> Beneath the radar of efficiency technicians and the stern disciples of instruc-
> tional approaches based on strict Skinnerian controls, one still may find hu-
> mane and happy elementary schools, both large and small, within poor neigh-
> borhoods in which affectionate and confident and morally committed teachers
> do not view themselves as the floor managers for industry whose job it is to
> pump some "added value" in undervalued children but who come into this
> very special world of miniature joys and miniature griefs out of their fascina-
> tion and delight with growing children and are thoroughly convinced that each
> and everyone [sic] of them has an inherent value to begin with.[6]

Let us not forget that democracy, like education, is about people. A teacher who believes in democratic practice does so because even the most troublesome child has something positive to contribute to society. In a democratic school, we do not give up on students nor do we view students from a deficit perspective. What we see, instead, are students that will, in time, become the adults in an emerging political and social democracy.

In a democratic school, everything we do has ramifications for developing participants who think critically about life's decisions, consider issues of equity, and care about the humanity in all of us. Our democracy cannot remain static. Therefore, a dynamic and evolving republic depends on leaders who give back to the community. We have an obligation to develop these dispositions and to educate those who will become the next leaders of society.

The most effective democratic schools are those that support democratic dispositions throughout the school. With the principal on board and other faculty working toward the same goals, there is no limit to what can take place. Teaching schedules can have dedicated time for teachers to meet and plan with other teachers. The possibility of interdisciplinary teaching increases. Professional development focuses on successes and barriers to democratic practice. Students are acknowledged not just for academic achievement but also for signs of caring or recognizing matters of school and society that reflect issues of social justice. According to Ayers, "Teachers and principals should not permit the beautiful profession they have chosen to be redefined by those who know far less than they about the hearts of children."[7]

We know that democratic practice is not straightforward. As Ayers notes, "Teachers need to be aware of the stakes, aware as well that there is no simple technique or linear path that will take them to where they need to go, and then allow them to live out their comfortable teaching lives, untroubled, settled, and finished. There is no promised land in teaching, just aching and persistent tension between reality and possibility."[8]

How do we communicate this quintessential idea to bright, eager pre-service teachers? How do we help pre-service teachers enter the urban teaching field and not experience the paralysis of culture shock? They need at least two things: (a) teacher educators with a realistic understanding of urban schooling, and (b) plenty of field experiences that give opportunities to develop productive relationships with the students.

With this foundation, pre-service teachers can begin to craft a philosophy of teaching that is practical for the urban school. They will have participated in communities of learning, knowing that such communities take time and hard work to function effectively. They understand the value of communities of inquiry among teachers themselves. And, they recognize that teaching for democratic practice involves moral responsibilities to ensure that students have excellent instruction, a culturally responsive curriculum, and access to resources that enrich the learning experience.

For teacher educators, the task of preparing students for urban teaching may seem monumental. "Although teacher educators alone cannot bring about political and social movements that are needed to alter the pathology of urban schools, they can at least educate teacher candidates to be aware of the situation so they enter schools with some understanding of the forces shaping people's behavior and the role they can play in the struggle to reform the pathology."[9] Herein lies the significance of good urban field placements, for it is the work of exemplary urban educators that reveals the small but substantial steps it takes to bring about change in the classroom and the school.

Under ideal circumstances, school-based democracy is a consequence of administrators, teachers, students, and members of the community working toward goals of democratic purpose. Fortunately, there are urban schools in this country that exemplify this level of support for democratic practice. Yet we know it is a huge undertaking that requires the coming together of minds from a variety of stakeholders.

Whether or not the school chooses to follow democratic goals, the teacher can still become a change agent in his/her own classroom. There is nothing to suggest that democracy leads to unbounded freedom of students. Democratic practice does not mean that teachers sacrifice content, or testing requirements, through small-group work and critical thinking tasks. Nor does democratic practice imply subversive action to undermine school policies.

Democratic practice involves the expectation that students must behave with civility in order to work together for the greater good. It requires a teacher who capitalizes on teachable moments and searches for the best ways of communicating content to students of different cultures. Democratic practice seeks to develop the students' sensitivity to inequities, whether in the school or the society, and the potential for following acceptable paths toward change.

Democracy when practiced assiduously is always in a state of becoming. Teaching for democratic practice, then, demands a particular mind-set on the part of the teacher. Teachers must not only embrace the concept of works in progress but also the discomfort of substantive chaos in the classroom as students struggle with challenging problems. As Beane and Apple remind us, "Democratic educators seek not simply to lessen the harshness of social inequities in school, but to change the conditions that create them."[10]

There is a difference between good schools and good democratically based schools. It is the voice in the back of our head that calls us to task when our curriculum does not fairly represent the diversity of our society. It is the perseverance with which we sludge through day after day of cranky, complaining students, knowing that working together is difficult but essential to a fully functioning society. It is the central belief that schools have a larger purpose than good teaching—that democratic practice gives students the tools and hope toward a life of innumerable choices and the "pursuit of happiness."

> June 15: *On awards night, Mei Hui stepped up to the microphone and, with grace and poise, spoke to the audience about her music teacher who was about to return to the university. She showed the audience a vase of flowers that she had beautifully crafted from pieces of tissue paper and presented it to me in the midst of resounding applause. Democratic practice was the furthest thing from my mind at that moment. I thought only about the students I was about to leave. For in the end, urban students do have caring hearts and souls despite their tough talk. Our job is to uncover the layers of defense and hurt to find the child within who loves to learn and learns to love.*

NOTES

1. Nicholas M. Michelli, "Democracy and Social Justice: What Can They Be?" Centre for Governance and Citizenship Working Paper Series No. 2011/002 (The Hong Kong Institute of Education, January 2011), 5. http://www.ied.edu.hk/cgc/view.php?secid=900.

2. William Ayers, "Teaching In and For Democracy," *Curriculum and Teaching Dialogue* 12, no. 1/2 (January 1, 2010): 5.

3. Michelli, "Democracy and Social Justice," 6.

4. Jeffrey M. R. Duncan-Andrade and Ernest Morrell, *The Art of Critical Pedagogy: Possibilities for Moving from Theory to Practice in Urban Schools* (New York: Peter Lang, 2008), 7.

5. Elaine M. Stotko, Rochelle Ingram, and Mary Ellen Beatty-O'Ferrall, "Promising Strategies for Attracting and Retaining Successful Urban Teachers," *Urban Education* 42, no. 1 (January 2007): 42. doi: 10.1177/0042085906293927.

6. Jonathan Kozol, *The Shame of the Nation* (NY: Three Rivers Press, 2005), 285–286.

7. Kozol, *Shame of the Nation,* 299.

8. William Ayers, "Teaching In and For Democracy," 10.

9. Christopher Ward Ellsasser, "Teaching Educational Philosophy: A Response to the Problem of First-Year Urban Teacher Transfer," *Urban Education* 40 (2008): 479. doi: 10.1177/0013124507304690.

10. James A. Beane and Michael W. Apple, "The Case for Democratic Schools," in *Democratic Schools,* ed. Michael W. Apple and James A. Beane (Alexandria, VA: Association for Supervision and Curriculum Development, 1995), 103.

Epilogue

William Grant Stills High School continued for three more years. Each year it added a new ninth grade class, excellent teachers, and more space in the upper-level floors. In those three years the school flourished, the students thrived, and the original cohort of students graduated with a newfound sense of competence and pride. In hindsight it is clear that the first year, chronicled in this book, served an important purpose. It taught us what we needed to develop a good school. Moreover, the lessons learned during its infancy contributed substantially to the powerful learning community that the school was to become.

The greatest of these lessons centered on the idea that a democratic school cannot function without community building on many different levels. In future years, the university and faculty would work tirelessly to bring students and teachers together. A summer bridge program for incoming freshman, for example, helped ease the transition between middle school and high school. Students benefited not only from progressive, challenging learning projects but also from a new network of friends including upperclassmen who served as student mentors from WGS. Thus, faculty and students started the academic year with a caring community already in progress.

That each member (e.g., students, faculty, parents, university) felt valued, through joint decision making and town meetings, contributed significantly to the school's systemic growth. WGS extended its community to the middle school where students met on Saturdays to learn literacy strategies for reading to young children. The school also became a laboratory for student teachers to observe and explore what it means to teach in a democratic setting. In essence the school had reached a point where its original vision—to create a high school for preparing adolescents for a teaching career—began to blossom. These initiatives suggested, then, that democratic practice was *not* the end in itself but a means toward achieving the mission of the school.

However, one voice—that of the district administration—was noticeably absent throughout. The lack of support from upper-level district administration would prove to have devastating consequences. What started out as a partnership between the university and the school district lapsed into a situation in which the school district actively sabotaged the school's increasing success.

At first it was small things, such as not distributing graphic calculators until after the state math tests or delaying or not providing other critical resources. The new chemistry lab, for instance, required an exhaust fan, but the district installed the fan on an interior rather than exterior wall, rendering the fan useless. Then the school was cited for numerous fire code regulations and temporarily closed down, forcing students and faculty to relocate to another building. The cumulative effect of these and other tactics slowed the wheels of change considerably. Perhaps the greatest damage occurred when the administration began to assign the best and brightest teacher applicants to other schools in the district despite the fact that they applied specifically for a position at WGS.

A democratic school cannot survive if one of its stakeholders systematically undermines the process. When this happens, there are no happy choices, as decisions are no longer made with the students' best interests at heart. Inevitably the partnership dissolved causing the school, as it was, to disband. In effect, WGS disappeared only to resurface as yet another inner-city school mired in administrative directives.

Was it worth it? Some would think so, others might disagree. Here's what the students said: "Our teachers won't let us fail. They seek you out if you are struggling. They work hard to help us meet their expectations. This school is a family." And, in the end, the faculty had found a way so that each graduating student (those from that first year) was able to complete an application for community college or university. Schooling now had special meaning for these students.

Five years after the birth of the school, as I walked past the university library, I happened to see a group of students approaching me with big smiles. They were my students from that very first cohort who had just been accepted to the university. We hugged as they excitedly told me about the wonderful experiences they had had at WGS. Moments later, I watched those four confident, enthusiastic teens run to class. WGS had served a critical role in helping them move beyond the streets. For them, life was just beginning.

www.ingramcontent.com/pod-product-compliance
Lightning Source LLC
Chambersburg PA
CBHW021820270326
41932CB00007B/268